Patternmaking
for Dress Design

BLOOMSBURY VISUAL ARTS
Bloomsbury Publishing Plc
50 Bedford Square, London, WC1B 3DP, UK
1385 Broadway, New York, NY 10018, USA
29 Earlsfort Terrace, Dublin 2, Ireland

BLOOMSBURY, BLOOMSBURY VISUAL ARTS and the Diana logo are trademarks of
Bloomsbury Publishing Plc

First published in Great Britain 2021

A catalogue record for this book is available from the British Library.

Library of Congress Cataloging-in-Publication Data
Names: Vanderlinde, Pamela, author.
Title: Patternmaking for dress design : 9 iconic styles from empire
to cheongsam / Pamela Vanderlinde.
Description: London ; New York : Bloomsbury Visual Arts, 2021. |
Includes bibliographical references and index.
Identifiers: LCCN 2021006010 (print) | LCCN 2021006011 (ebook) | ISBN 9781350094673
(paperback) | ISBN 9781350094697 (pdf) | ISBN 9781350235946 (ebook)
Subjects: LCSH: Dressmaking–Pattern design.
Classification: LCC TT520 .V36 2021 (print) | LCC TT520 (ebook) | DDC 646.4–dc23
LC record available at https://lccn.loc.gov/2021006010
LC ebook record available at https://lccn.loc.gov/2021006011

ISBN: PB: 978-1-3500-9467-3
          ePDF: 978-1-3500-9469-7
          eBook: 978-1-3502-3594-6

Typeset by Integra Software Services Pvt. Ltd.
Printed and bound in India

To find out more about our authors and books visit www.bloomsbury.com
and sign up for our newsletters.

Patternmaking for Dress Design

9 Iconic Styles from
Empire to Cheongsam

Pamela Vanderlinde

BLOOMSBURY VISUAL ARTS
LONDON · NEW YORK · OXFORD · NEW DELHI · SYDNEY

Contents

Preface

As a designer, I have always been intrigued as to why any specific style endures the test of time. What is it in its history that continues to lead designers to use it as a form of inspiration? Whether these pieces are used as a direct reference or just implied, they seem to set the theme for entire collections. My fascination led to writing my first text, *Patternmaking for Jacket and Coat Design*, which focused on the historical relevance and patternmaking of seven iconic jackets and coats. Feeling that there was more to uncover in the history of garment design, I continued my journey into the whys of fashion and began to research iconic dresses.

Patternmaking for Dress Design offers a comprehensive, project-based approach to the patternmaking techniques for nine iconic dress designs as inspirations for contemporary fashion. Each chapter is devoted to a historically significant design. Each chapter illustrates the history and relevance of one design, and gives examples of how it has influenced and inspired designers today.

For each project, detailed step-by-step instructions with corresponding illustrations guide the drafting of the complete pattern. Photographs of each dress are included at both the muslin or toile and final fitting stage, along with technical flats to show the design details. The dresses depicted in this book are meant to be used as inspiration only, and are not historical replicas. This allows the student/designer to branch out creatively and use these projects as reference in future designs.

My goal in writing this book was to combine my love of fashion, dress design, and its history in a patternmaking text that would be approachable, easy to understand, and hopefully just a bit thought-provoking. Now more than ever we need to rethink dress and what it means to society. My methodology of design is to create pieces that can be worn for a lifetime, a system of sustainability that is centuries old. The dresses I chose for this book represent silhouettes that have endured the test of time and are as relevant today as when they first appeared.

At work in the studio.

Introduction: Block Development

Patterning concepts learned

- Front torso block with side-bust dart
- Front and back contouring principles

"Design is not for philosophy, it's for life."
Issey Miyake

Patternmaking Fundamentals

There are three types of patternmaking used in the fashion industry: pattern drafting, draping, and flat patterning. The flat-pattern method relies on the manipulation of blocks (also called slopers) to develop the pattern for any given design. Every patternmaker will have their own set of blocks with which they create these designs. These blocks will correlate with the sample size for their intended target market within the industry.

In this section I have included directions to modify the basic bodice, torso, and sleeve blocks, along with contouring principles that are necessary to pattern the dresses outlined in the book. I have not included the instructions for drafting the basic block set because those blocks must directly correspond to the dress form. Having a good set of blocks is critical in flat pattern-making—without them it would be impossible to fit the garment accurately at all stages of the design process.

You will also need to develop contouring guidelines for the torso and bodice blocks. Contouring of the pattern is necessary so there is no gaping around the neckline and armholes when creating new designs. Contour guidelines are included in this section for the torso and bodice blocks.

If you do not have a set of basic blocks, you will need to draft or drape them according to the measurements of the form you are using. There are many patternmaking books that will aid you in the development of these blocks, and some are listed in the Bibliography of this book. Drafting the basic blocks can be time consuming and a difficult task to undertake if patternmaking is somewhat new to you. Draping is a much more efficient and accurate method for creating your basic blocks, as you have a form to work with instead of just measurements. Commercial pattern companies also have basic block patterns that you can purchase, which include directions on how to fit and adjust to individual body types. These are usually called a "missy's fitting shell." This is a good option if you need to make blocks for yourself or others and do not have a dress form that matches the corresponding measurements.

Once you have developed the blocks illustrated here, you will have not only the patterns necessary to develop the nine projects outlined in the book but also the patternmaking tools and concepts needed to design your own unique creations.

AUTHOR TIP

Patternmaking terminology is covered in the Glossary section of the book.

A sizing chart for drafting the basic block set has not been included because blocks must directly correspond to the dress form. The Bibliography lists patternmaking books that will aid in the development of blocks.

Both imperial and metric measurements are included in the instructions, so there is no need for a conversion chart.

Basic bodice, torso, skirt, and sleeve blocks

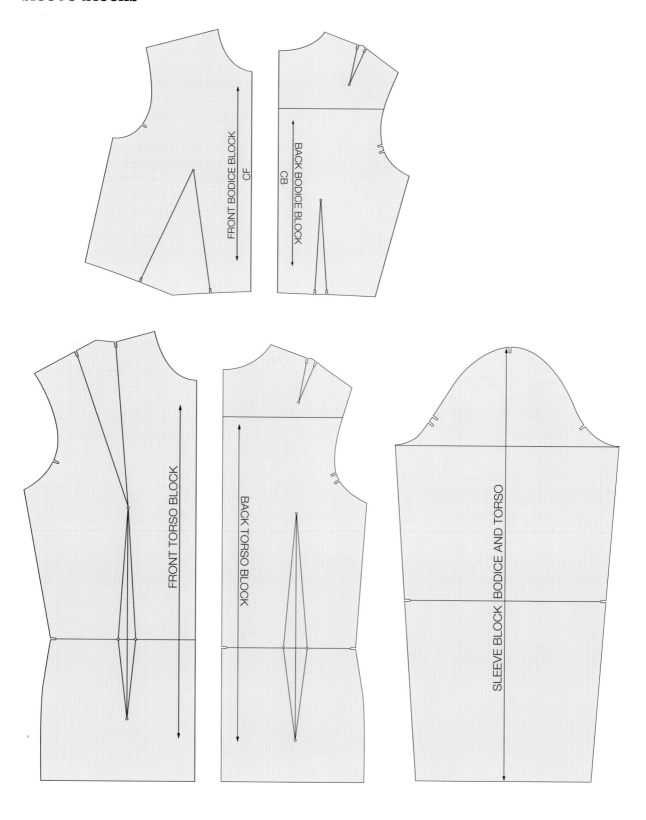

FRONT BODICE BLOCK
CF

BACK BODICE BLOCK
CB

FRONT TORSO BLOCK

BACK TORSO BLOCK

SLEEVE BLOCK BODICE AND TORSO

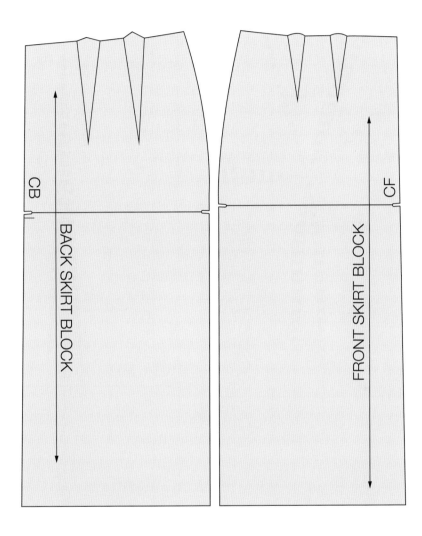

CB

BACK SKIRT BLOCK

CF

FRONT SKIRT BLOCK

Torso contour blocks

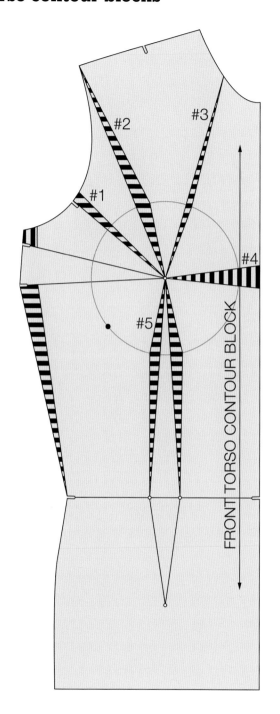

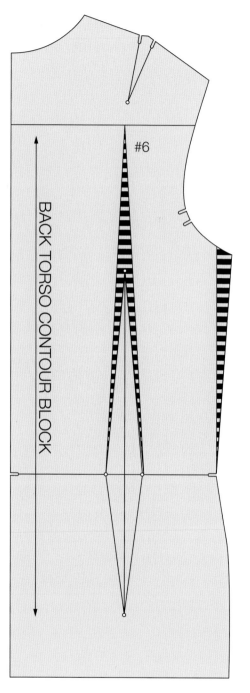

Contouring guidelines

Contouring of the bodice and torso blocks is necessary (shaded areas) when changing the shape of the neckline and/or armholes. The basic blocks have ease built into them, and this needs to be adjusted to allow the garment to lie properly on contours of the body. The removal of this ease can be achieved by using the basic contour guidelines outlined here. First you must transfer the shoulder dart to the side-seam in order to get the torso block ready for the guidelines.

Whenever your style line passes through a contouring line, you must transfer excess ease into the side-bust dart to control the fit. Measurements given here are standardized, so use them only as a guide. The amount of adjustment necessary depends on bust size. Always do a test fit of your pattern in muslin to ensure you are happy with the contouring before you move on to fashion fabric.

Guidelines for contouring are numbered on the block, and their functions are explained below.

Guideline 1: Armhole ease
Guideline 2: Armhole ease
Guideline 3: Cut-away neckline
Guidelines 1–3 combined: Strapless designs
Guideline 4: Contour between busts (cleavage)
Guideline 5: Empire line
Guideline 6: Strapless and halter designs (back pattern)

AUTHOR TIP

Contour guidelines are only shown for the torso block, but the same principles apply when using the bodice block. You will transfer excess ease into the waist dart.

Blocks Manipulated
Front torso block with side-bust dart block
Transferring shoulder dart to side-seam

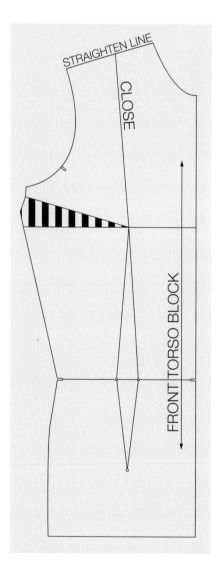

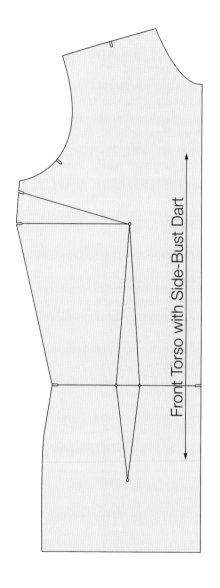

1. Trace front torso block.
2. Move shoulder dart to the side-seam using the slash-and-spread method.
3. Draw a slash line perpendicular to the center front (CF) passing through the bust point (apex).
4. Cut slash line to the edge of the bust point (apex).
5. Cut shoulder dart leg to the edge of the bust point (apex).
6. Close shoulder dart and tape shut.
7. Straighten shoulder if necessary.v

Front torso contour block

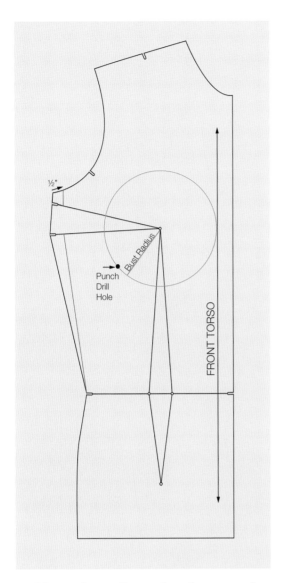

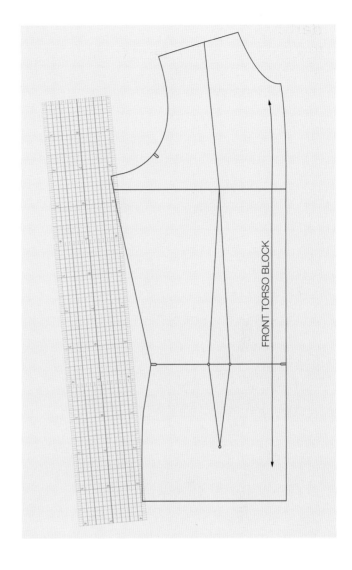

1. Measure bust radius on dress form, record_____.
   Note: To measure the bust radius, place a tape measure on the bust point (apex) and measure the distance to the edge of the bust.
2. Trace front torso block with side-dart.
3. Place compass at bust point (apex) and, using radius measurement, draw bust circumference.
4. Place a drill hole on the circle to use when transferring the contouring lines of the block to the pattern.
5. Mark ½ inch (1.2 cm) in at side-seam at underarm and draw a guideline from the waist. This will eliminate ease for strapless and halter garments. **Note: It is easier to do this guideline with the side-bust dart closed.**

6. You will fold dart excess towards the waistline.
7. Score the dart leg with an awl closest to the direction in which you are folding the dart.
8. Close the pattern by placing the dart point on the side corner of the table and matching up the dart legs as if you were sewing them, and tape down.
9. Place ruler on the block and mark your ½ inch (1.2 cm) guideline as shown. **Note: Do not cut this guideline out on block!**

Contour guideline 1

Contour guideline 2

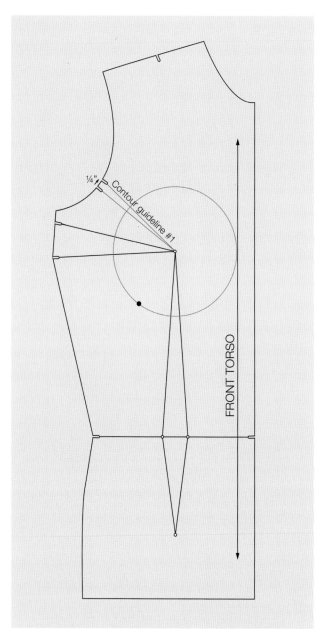

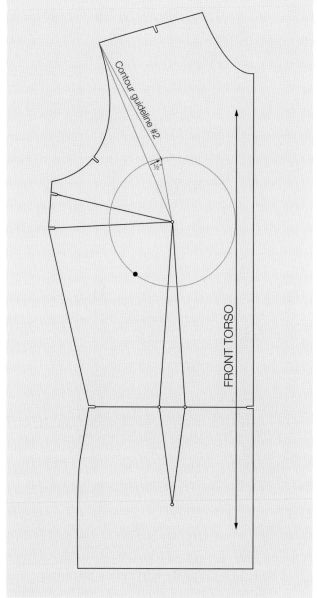

Contour guideline 1 helps to eliminate gaping in the armhole when a garment has a cut-away or strapless design.

1. Draw a guideline from the bust point (apex) to the front armhole notch.
2. Mark ¼ inch (6 mm) up from guideline and connect to apex.
3. Mark this #1 on the pattern.

Contour guideline 2 helps to eliminate gaping in the armhole when a garment has a cut-away, strapless, or halter/racerback design.

1. Draw a guideline from the bust point (apex) to the shoulder tip.
2. Mark ½ inch (1.2 cm) toward CF on bust circumference.
3. Draw a slanted guideline connecting apex to circumference mark to shoulder tip.

Contour guideline 3

Contour guideline 4

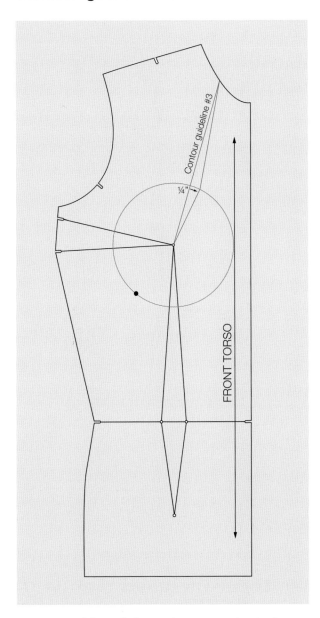

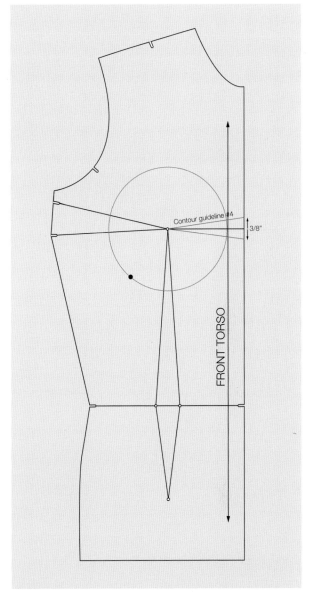

Contour guideline 3 helps to eliminate gaping in the neckline when a garment has a lowered neckline design. It also eliminates gaping in strapless designs.

1. Draw a guideline from the bust point (apex) to the mid-neck.
2. Mark ¼ inch (6 mm) toward CF on bust circumference.
3. Draw a slanted guideline connecting apex to circumference mark to mid-neck.

Contour guideline 4 helps to eliminate gaping when there is contouring between busts (cleavage), such as plunging necklines, strapless, and wrap designs.

1. Square a guideline from CF to apex (bust point).
2. Mark two points 3/8 inch (1 cm) out from guideline and connect to apex.

Contour guideline 5

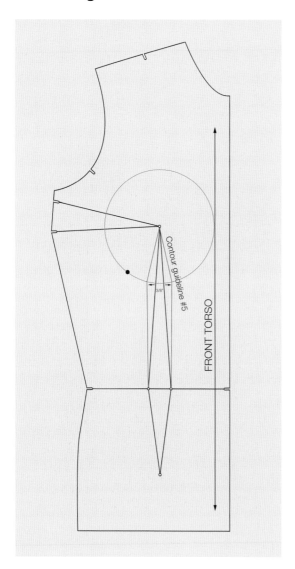

Back torso contour block
Contour guideline 6

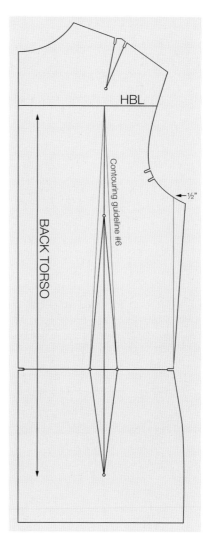

Contour guideline 5 is used for Empire-style designs.

1. Mark two points 3/8 inch (1 cm) out from bust dart at circumference.
2. Draw slanted guideline connecting bust point (apex) to circumference marks to waistline.

Contour guideline 6 is used for strapless and cut-out-neckline designs.

1. Trace back torso block.
2. Extend mid-point of back waistline dart to the horizontal balance line (HBL).
3. Draw guidelines from waist dart to HBL.
4. Mark ½ inch (1.2 cm) in at side-seam at underarm and draw a guideline from the waist. This will eliminate ease for strapless and halter garments. **Note: Do not cut this guideline out on block!**

Front and back bodice contour blocks

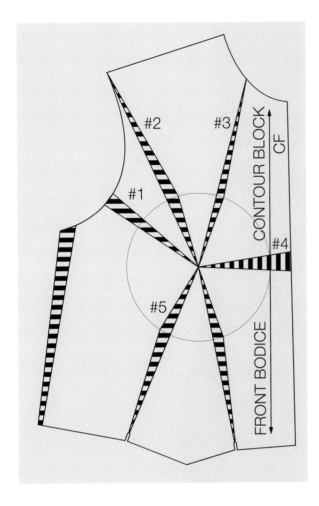

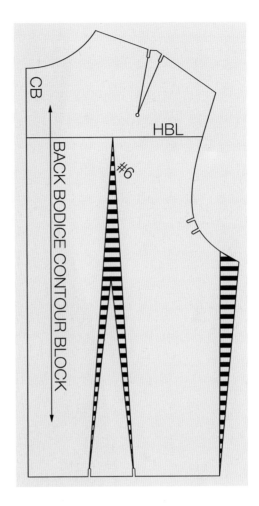

To create bodice contour blocks, transfer the guidelines from the front and back torso contour blocks on to the front and back bodice blocks.

Seam Allowances

The following information is a general guideline for allowances used for patternmaking in the professional garment industry.

1/4 inch (6 mm)

- All faced areas (enclosed seams)
- Sleeveless armholes
- Narrow spacing
- Extreme curves
- Necklines

- Down CF in a blouse/jacket/coat
- Collars, lapels

1/2 inch (1.2 cm)

- Armholes with sleeves
- Waistlines
- Style lines
- Side-seams
- Zipper seams (with the exception of separating and lapped zippers)
- CF lines in skirts/pants

The Empire-waist Dress

Patterning concepts learned

- Empire waistline
- Bodice armhole contouring
- Flared gored skirt
- All-in-one facing
- Lining patterns

Figure 1.1
Designed Empire-waist dress.

The History of the Empire-waist dress

It is said that the Empire-waist dress, also known as the Empire line, with its neoclassical inspirations, was first popularized by Empress Josephine, Napoleon's wife, in the early nineteenth century. She often described her entourage as a "Court of Gods and Goddesses," and the style, which was fitted under the bust and draped loosely like garments on Greek and Roman statues, helped to give this illusion. Corsets were temporarily abandoned in favor of the natural figure, and this shift in style is thought to be the end result of the French Revolution and the break with aristocracy. The neoclassical style made it across the Channel to England during this time and was termed the Regency style, referring to the regency of the Prince of Wales, who ruled from 1811 to 1820 before becoming king. The thin muslin sheath dress was most often worn in a shade of white—this helped to project the wearers' superior social status, as only women of a higher class could afford a wardrobe that so easily became dirtied.

Figure 1.3
Postcard depicting a woman wearing a hobble skirt, 1911.

Figure 1.2
Portrait of Josephine as Venus by Andrea Appiani, 1796.

But Napoleon's rule was as short-lived as the style, and by 1825, ten years after his final defeat at the Battle of Waterloo, fashion had transitioned to a new "romantic" look with the bodice ending just a few inches above the natural waistline. Thus began another hundred years of corseting women. But throughout the twentieth century numerous film and television adaptations set during the Regency period helped to keep the Empire-line dress in the mind's eye and a relevant fashion choice; and novels by Jane Austen and the Brontë sisters written during the Regency era prove to be just as popular today as they were back in the early nineteenth century.

The first renaissance of the Empire line occurred in the early part of the twentieth century, with Italian designer Mariano Fortuny's Delphos gown. Inspired by ancient Greek styles, the pleated silk gown became popular amongst artists and the more unconventional affluent women of the time. The dress takes its name from the bronze statue of the Charioteer of Delphi (created 475–470 BC), and intricately emulates the folds in the charioteer's tunic, with miniscule pleats falling from the shoulders to puddle at the floor. Even though the dress lacked a true Empire line, it was generally tied under the bust, thus giving it the same effect. The first Delphos was presented in 1907, and it continued to be produced until shortly after Fortuny's death in 1949. Today, vintage versions of the dress have become collectors' items and sell for thousands of dollars.

A more modest version of the neoclassical Empire-line dress became fashionable around 1909, just a few years after Fortuny's introduction of the Delphos. During this time the bodice styles were simplified, with close-fitting sleeves, either full length or ending below the elbow, and narrow full-length skirts. Some of the skirts were so narrow that it was problematic to walk in them, and became known as hobble skirts due to the difficulty of movement while wearing them. This was the era when Paul Poiret famously claimed to have liberated women from the corset, but in fact the revival of the Empire-line style demanded a new type of underpinning combined with a straight-waisted corset that helped to achieve the slender silhouette fashionable at the time.

In the 1960s Empire waists made yet another appearance and were a common look for both the conservative crowd and the youth movement, at the time known as hippies. The hippie counterculture movement got its start on college campuses in the United States and was known for its slogan of "make love, not war." Hippies removed themselves from mainstream conventions, and often looked to Eastern influences and yogic philosophies. Hippies got their name from the term "hip," which was a Beat-generation moniker for all things cool in the 1950s. Hippies protested against the war in Vietnam, gave up the conventional lifestyle of their parents' generation, and developed their own particular style. Both men and women grew their hair long and dressed themselves in thrift-store finds, or better yet wore homemade clothes reminiscent of the styles of the 1920s. The hippie style for women was often maxi-dresses cut in an Empire style and gathered with elastic at the neckline and under the bust. The mainstream also embraced the high-waisted look, but it was a more conservative fitted version that generally had a matching jacket or coat.

In 1995 a British TV adaptation of Jane Austen's novel *Pride and Prejudice*, set during the Regency era, made the Empire-line silhouette fashionable yet again, and the cut has continued to hold a place in fashion ever since.

Figure 1.4
Delphos gown designed by Mariano Fortuny.

Figure 1.5
Vietnam War protesters march at the Pentagon in Washington, DC, on October 21, 1967.

"It's not what we say or think but what we do that defines us."

Jane Austen

Contemporary Empire-waist Dresses

Designers show drastically different interpretations of the Empire line as seen on the catwalk.

Figure 1.6
Molly Goddard, Runway, London Fashion Week, February 2019.

Figure 1.7
Gucci, Runway, Milan Fashion Week, Spring/Summer 2020.

The Pattern

Start with front torso contour block and back torso blocks

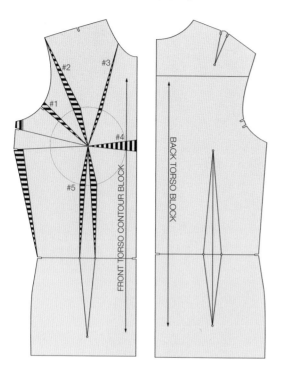

AUTHOR TIP

Directions for the front torso contour block can be found in the "Block Development" section of the Introduction to this book.

Lengthen pattern and front Empire style line

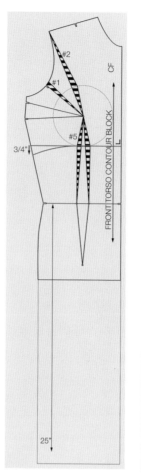

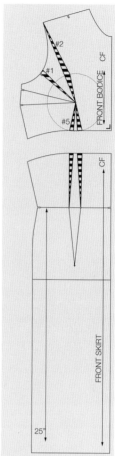

Contour guidelines needed

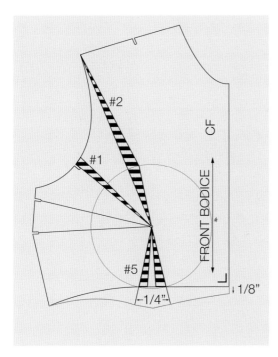

1. Trace front torso contour block, transferring guidelines 1, 2, and 5 on to your pattern.
2. Extend length 25 inches (62.5 cm) from waist. **Note: You can extend the length as much or as little as you prefer.**
3. Square a line parallel to center front (CF), using the bottom of the bust circumference as your reference point.
4. At side-seam, mark ¾ inch (1.75 cm) down from squared-off line.
5. Draw a curved line (red curved line) connecting side-seam at mark to contour guideline 5, as shown.
6. Cut pattern pieces apart.
7. Label front bodice and front skirt, retaining waist and hip notches on skirt.
8. Extend dart legs ¼ inch (6 mm) down and CF ⅛ inch (3 mm) down on bodice.
9. Draw a curved line (red curved line) to blend. **Note: This will allow for a better fit under the bust.**

Front racerback armhole development

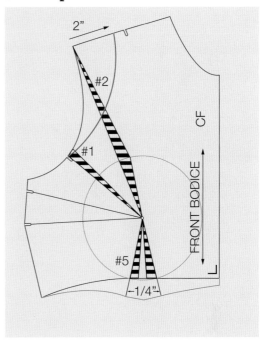

1. Move shoulder seam in 2 inches (5 cm) as shown.
2. Draw a curved line from the new shoulder point, stopping at the armhole notch (red curved line), for the racerback armhole.
3. Cut out new armhole.
4. Transfer contour guideline darts 1 and 2 and side-bust dart to the Empire bust contour guideline dart 5 using the slash-and-spread method.
5. Slash paper on these guidelines and on side-bust dart leg to bust point (apex).
6. Close guidelines and side-bust dart, and tape shut. **Note: The full intake for dart 2 will not completely close.**
7. Smooth out racerback armhole.
8. Smooth out side-seam if necessary.
9. Make sure to retain armhole notch.

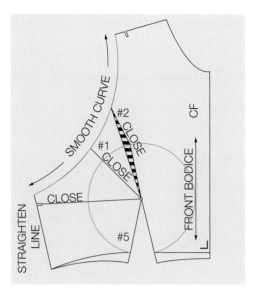

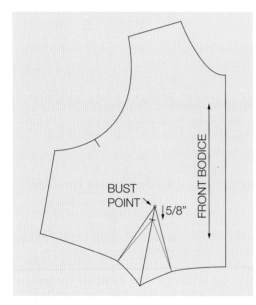

Lengthen pattern and draw back Empire style line

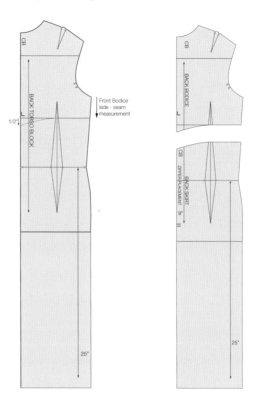

10. Find mid-point of dart intake and mark dart point ⅝ inch (1.5 cm) from bust point (apex).

11. Draw new dart legs, folding and closing the dart intake toward the CF. Make sure to fold the dart legs from the dart point and not the bust point (apex)!

1. Trace back torso block.
2. Extend length 25 inches (62.5 cm) from waist.
3. For back Empire line, square a line parallel to center back (CB) that equals the front bodice side-seam measurement.
4. At CB, mark ½ inch (1.2 cm) down from squared-off line.
5. Draw a curved line (red curved line) for the back Empire style line.
6. Cut pattern pieces apart.
7. True up dart legs if necessary.
8. Label back bodice and back skirt, retaining waist and hip notches on skirt.
9. Mark a double notch 7 inches (17.5 cm) down from waist at CB for zipper placement. **Note: You must always have a double notch someplace on a back pattern piece.**

Back racerback armhole development

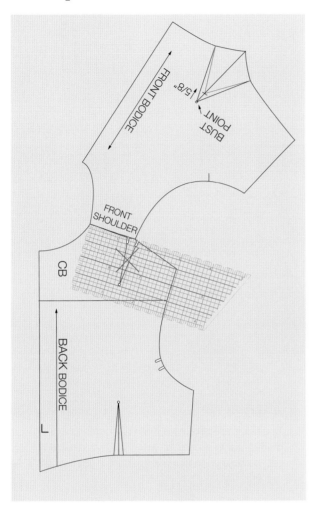

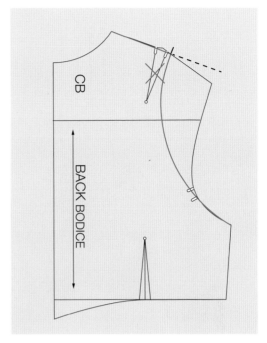

1. For the back racerback style line, you must first eliminate the back shoulder dart.
2. Place ruler even with shoulder line at neckline, and draw a straight line that equals the front shoulder measurement.
3. Draw a curved line from new shoulder point, stopping at the armhole notch for the new armhole. **Note: The back shoulder dart has been technically "transferred" to the part of the armhole that will be cut out for the racerback (dotted line).**

Gored skirt

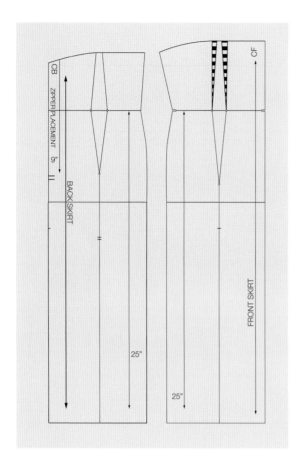

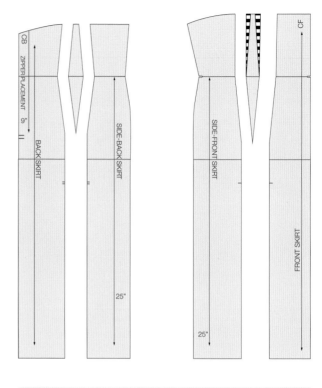

1. Extend cut line (red line) from contour dart point to hem parallel to CF and CB on both front and back skirt patterns.
2. Notch as shown and cut apart, making sure to cut out the darts.
3. Draw grain lines perpendicular to waist, and label as shown.

AUTHOR TIP

You want to make sure that your notches are distributed in such a way that you will be able to tell the difference between pattern pieces when sewing.

Flared gored skirt

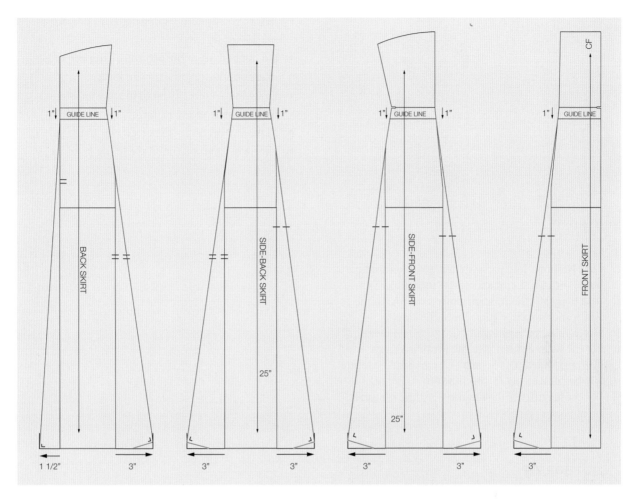

1. Trace skirt patterns.
2. Extend hemline out 3 inches (7.5 cm) and square up as shown.
3. Mark 1 inch (2.5 cm) below waistline.
4. Measure the distance from guideline to hem, and record_____.
5. Using the recorded measurement, place the ruler on the guideline and draw new seam, connecting it to the squared-off line at the hem.
6. Square the seam off until it meets up with the original hem.
7. Smooth out line if necessary.
8. Make the same pattern adjustments to seams, with the exception of the CF and CB.
9. Extend the CB seam 1½ inches (3.75 cm) or half of the flare measurement.
10. Do not flare the CF, as the pattern will be mirrored.
11. Make sure to transfer all darts to the new flared seams.

> **AUTHOR TIP**
>
> This new line appears shorter than the original because of the flare, but it is not. If you fail to adjust the new seam, the hemline will be uneven.

Wrap-around belt and belt loops

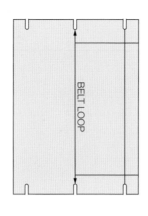

1. For belt loops, fold paper in half and square a line out ¾ inch (1.75 cm) and up 1½ inches (3.75 cm).
2. Add ½ inch (1.2 cm) seam allowance (SA) to the width and ¼ inch (6 mm) SA to the length.
3. Notch fold line as shown.
4. For the wrap-around belt, the width is ½ inch (1.2 cm) folded plus ½ inch (1.2 cm) SA. The fabric will be cut 2 inches (5 cm) in width.
5. For the length, use the Empire waistline measurement plus 60 inches (150 cm).

> **AUTHOR TIP**
>
> I have added SA here to simplify production pattern development.

Muslin or Toile Fitting

- Before you draft the lining patterns, prepare a muslin for fit.
- Do not add SA to the pattern, as you will most likely be adjusting the muslin for fit.
- Draw the SA directly on to the muslin after tracing the working pattern.
- Make any necessary fit corrections to the pattern.
- Now you can move on to the lining patterns.

Figure 1.9
Detail of muslin fitting.

Figure 1.8
Checking muslin fit.

Front and back bodice all-in-one facing and lining

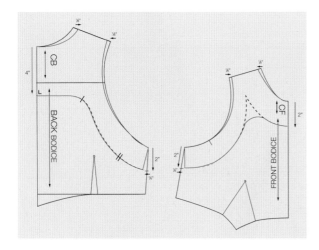

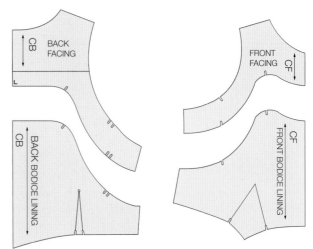

1. Trace front and back bodice patterns.
2. For the front bodice all-in-one facing, draw curved lines 2 inches (5 cm) around the neckline and armhole until lines intersect.
3. For the back bodice all-in-one facing, square a line 4 inches (10 cm) down from CB and mark 2 inches (5 cm) around the armhole until lines intersect.

4. Smooth out the pointy parts, as shown, for both front and back facings.
5. On facing pieces, reduce the shoulder seams, necklines, and bottom edge of the side-seams by ⅛ inch (3 mm), as shown, blending to the original seams. **Note: You need to reduce the facing pieces so they roll into the inside of the garment when sewn.**
6. Notch as shown and cut apart; label front facing, back facing, front bodice lining, and back bodice lining.

Front and back skirt lining

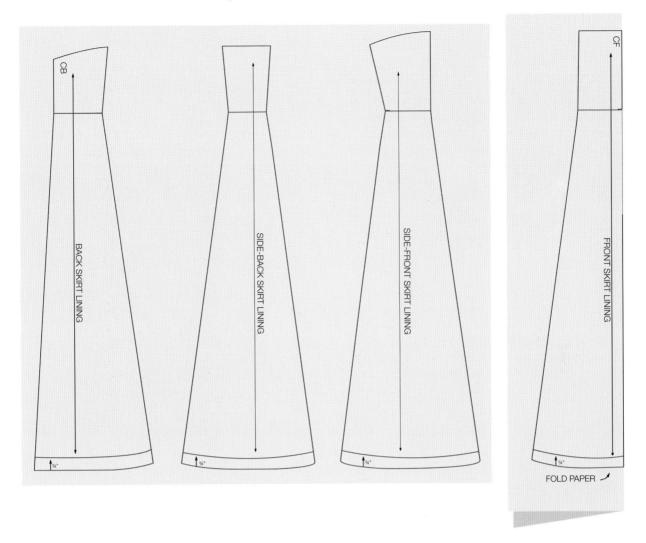

1. Fold paper in half and trace the front skirt pattern.
2. Trace side-front, back, and side-back skirt patterns.
3. Reduce hem ¾ inch (1.75 cm) on all pattern pieces.
4. Mark ¾ inch (1.75 cm) up from hemline.
5. Draw new hem and cut out excess.

Production Pattern
Seam allowances and hems

> **AUTHOR TIP**
>
> Before adding SAs and hems, be sure to walk your patterns and make any necessary corrections if seams and/or control notches do not match.

Front bodice, front facing, and front bodice lining seam allowances

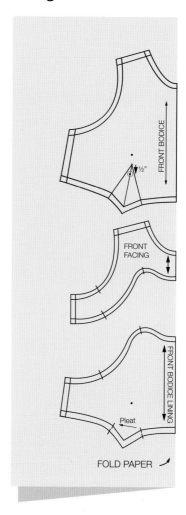

1. Fold paper in half and trace the front bodice, front facing, and front bodice lining.
2. Add ½ inch (1.2 cm) SA to seams for Empire waistline and shoulder, and side-seams.

Back bodice, back facing, and back bodice lining

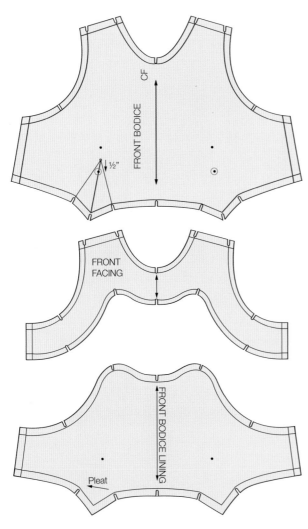

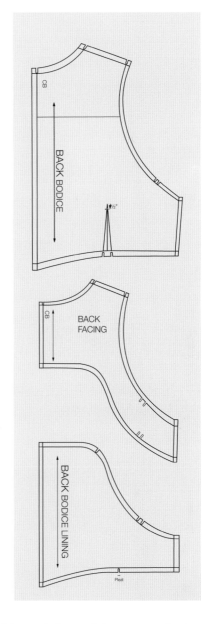

3. Add ¼ inch (6 mm) SA to front necklines, armholes, and where the front facing and front bodice lining are sewn together.
4. Circle and drill ½ inch (1.2 cm) into front bodice dart.
5. The dart in the front bodice lining becomes a pleat.
6. Cut patterns out.
7. Notch patterns as shown while patterns are still folded.

1. Add ½ inch (1.2 cm) SA to seams for Empire waistline, shoulder, and back, and side-seams.
2. Add ¼ inch (6 mm) SA to back necklines, armholes, and where the back facing and back bodice lining are sewn together.
3. Circle and drill ½ inch (1.2 cm) into back bodice dart.
4. The dart in the back bodice lining becomes a pleat.
5. Notch patterns as shown.

Front skirt, side-front skirt, back and side-back seam allowances and hems

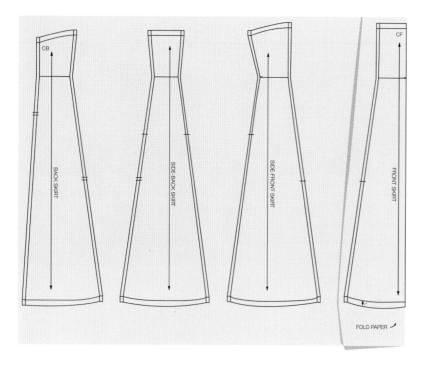 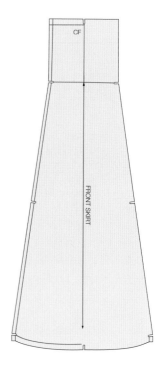

1. Fold paper in half and trace front skirt pattern.
2. Add ½ inch (1.2 cm) SA to all seams.
3. Add 1 inch (2.5 cm) SA for hem.
4. Notch patterns as shown, notching the front while still folded.

Front skirt lining, side-front skirt lining, back skirt lining, and side-back skirt lining seam allowances and hems

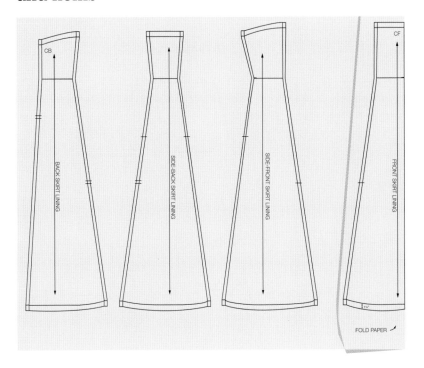
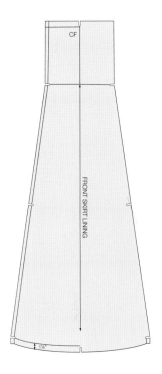

1. Fold paper in half and trace front skirt pattern.
2. Add ½ inch (1.2 cm) SA to all seams.
3. Add 1¼ inches (3 cm) to hem. This will allow the lining to hang ¾ inch (1.75 cm) above skirt hem on the finished garment.
4. Notch patterns as shown, notching the front while still folded.

TECHNICAL FLATS AND FINISHED PATTERN PIECES

Technical flat front

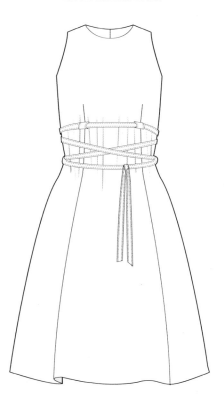

Technical flat back

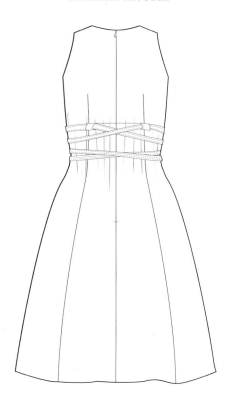

Self
Front bodice (cut 1)
Back bodice (cut 2)
Front skirt (cut 1)
Back skirt (cut 2)
Front facing (cut 1)
Back facing (cut 2)
Belt loop (cut 2)
Belt (cut 1)

Interfacing
Front facing (cut 1)
Back facing (cut 2)
Belt loop (cut 2)

Lining
Front bodice (cut 1)
Back bodice (cut 2)
Front skirt (cut 1)
Back skirt (cut 2)

> "The weight of the world is love. Under the burden of solitude, under the burden of dissatisfaction."
>
> Allen Ginsberg

Figure 1.10
Waistline detail.

The Sheath Dress

Patterning concepts learned

- Armhole princess style line
- Bateau neckline
- Bandeau collar
- Pegged/pencil skirt
- Lapped zipper
- Back vent
- Bias-bound armhole
- Lining patterns

Figure 2.1
Designed sheath dress.

The History of the Sheath

The sheath dress, most commonly associated with Audrey Hepburn and the 1961 film *Breakfast at Tiffany's*, is considered one of the most iconic pieces of clothing designed in the twentieth century. Hubert de Givenchy gets credit for the dress that made the phrase famous, but the original "little black dress" was actually presented by Coco Chanel decades before, in 1926. It is important to note that her version was not actually a sheath but a shift; more on that below.

A staple in most wardrobes, the sheath with its simple princess style lines and form-fitting shape is the quintessential cocktail dress. The sheath is often confused with the shift dress, which has a more relaxed fit that just skims the body. The shift was first made fashionable during the flapper era, and its popularity is credited to the designer Paul Poiret. The sheath's fit is created by the use of long panels that hug the body to ensure a snug fit. The dress can be traced back far before the early twentieth century: images from ancient

Figure 2.3
Alexandra of Denmark, who later became the Princess of Wales, in 1889

Figure 2.2
Egyptian statue wearing sleeved tunic, 151–150 BC.

Egyptian artwork depict women of all classes wearing a wrapped piece of fabric worn under a fitted beaded net dress. This is commonly referred to as the first sheath.

The princess line, which gives the dress its sleek fit, is said to have been conceived by Charles Frederick Worth in the 1870s and named in honor of the Princess of Wales, who later became Queen Alexandra. Alix, as she was known to those close to her, and her husband Bertie were known for their lavish parties and sense of style. They stood out amongst the fashion elite and informed the styles of the day. Bertie, who later became King Edward VII, also had his fair share of fashion moments. It was his Savile Row tailor Henry Poole who, at the prince's request, famously cut off the tails from his evening coat, thus originating what is known today as the tuxedo.

In 1950 Christian Dior introduced the "Vertical Line" collection based on the princess line, and referred to the sheath as the "slim look for five o'clock on." *Vogue* magazine called Dior's version of the sheath "the most important day in fashion." The close-fitting form was in direct contrast to his feminine, flirty "New Look" from just a few seasons earlier, and took the fashion world by storm. It is said that he named it a cocktail dress in reference to the American lifestyle, where, for the fashionable, cocktails were served every day at 5.00 pm sharp.

The sheath continued to be a hit well into the next decade, and at times these dresses were so narrow that they were termed pencil dresses and a vent or kick pleat was needed to allow the wearer to walk. These exaggerated versions were also referred to as "wiggle dresses." The most famous of the wiggle dresses has to be the one that Marilyn Monroe donned in 1962 when she sang "Happy Birthday" to President John F. Kennedy. The crystal-encrusted nude-colored sheath designed by Jean Louis was so tight that she had to be sewn into it. It was quite a scandal at the time, as it was rumored that the president and Ms Monroe were having an affair. The dress has lived on in infamy, and in 2016 was sold for $4.8 million at auction. The president's wife, Jackie, was also a famous wearer of a more modest and refined version.

Season after season, a version of the sheath will show up in some iteration in most designers' collections. The little black dress continues to be the go-to essential in most fashionable closets.

Figure 2.4
Actress Marilyn Monroe sings "Happy Birthday" to President John F. Kennedy at Madison Square Garden for his upcoming 45th birthday in 1962.

Figure 2.5
Actress Audrey Hepburn as Holly Golightly in the film *Breakfast at Tiffany's*, 1961.

> "When you don't dress like everybody else, you don't have to think like everybody else."
>
> Iris Apfel

Contemporary Sheaths

Two distinctive interpretations of the sheath dress show the variety of ways designers incorporate this iconic silhouette in modern ways.

Figure 2.6
Slava Zaitsev Fashion Laboratory, Mercedes-Benz Fashion Week, Autumn/Winter 2019/2020'
gettyimages-1134154373-594x594

Figure 2.7
Alexander McQueen, Runway, Paris Fashion Week, Fall/Winter 2018/2019.

The Pattern

Start with front torso with side-bust dart and back blocks

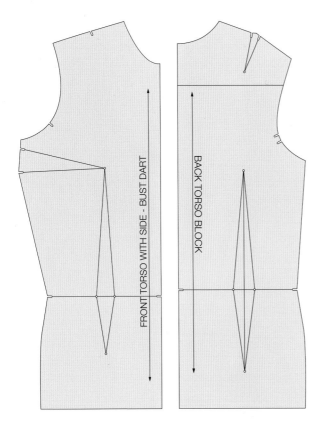

Front bateau neckline development and skirt pegging

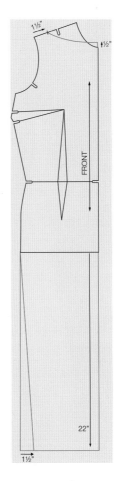

1. Trace front pattern.
2. Raise center front (CF) neckline by ½ inch (1.2 cm).
3. Move neckline out so shoulder measures 1½ inches (3.75 cm) from the shoulder tip and draw a slightly curved neckline, making sure to square off at CF.
4. Place contour template over front to determine if contouring is needed for this style line and adjust if necessary. **Note: For this neckline, no adjustment is needed.**
5. Lengthen torso 22 inches (55 cm) or to desired length. **Note: Make sure to retain hip notch.**
6. To peg/pencil the skirt, decrease side-seams at the hemline by 1½ inches (3.75 cm) and draw a straight line to hip notch.

AUTHOR TIP

Patterning directions for the front torso with side-bust dart block are in the "Blocks Identified" section of the Introduction to this book.

Move back shoulder dart to armhole and skirt pegging

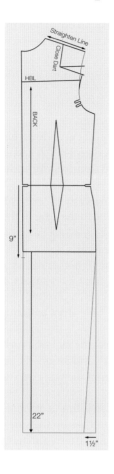

Back bateau neckline development and skirt vent

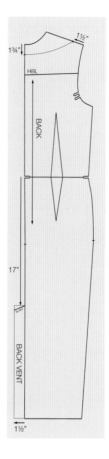

1. Trace back pattern.
2. For the back block transfer the shoulder dart to the armhole using the slash-and-spread method.
3. Square a slash line perpendicular to the center back (CB) from the shoulder dart point to the armhole.
4. Cut slash line to the edge of the dart point.
5. Cut shoulder dart leg to the edge of the dart point.
6. Close shoulder dart and tape shut.
7. True up armhole curve with a French curve.
8. Straighten shoulder line if not straight.
9. Lengthen torso 22 inches (55 cm) or to desired length. **Note: Make sure to retain hip notch.**
10. To peg/pencil the skirt, decrease side-seams at the hemline by 1½ inches (3.75 cm) and draw a straight line to hip notch.
11. Mark control notch 9 inches (22.5 cm) down from CB waist for zipper placement.

1. Lower CB neckline 1¾ inches (4.25 cm).
2. Move neckline out so shoulder measures 1½ inch (3.75 cm) from the shoulder tip and draw a slightly curved neckline, making sure to square off at CB (red line).
3. For back vent, mark down 17 inches (42.5 cm) from CB waist.
4. For back vent, measure out from CB 1½ inches (3.75 cm) and draw a line.
5. Draw a slanted line at top to connect.
6. Notch CB hemline.

Front princess style line

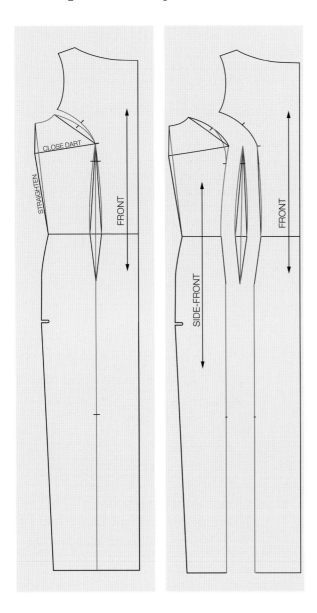

1. For the front block, draw a center line through the contour dart and extend down to hem.
2. Mark a control notch midway between waist and hem.
3. Draw a straight line from apex to armhole; draw a slight curve above.
4. Mark control notches 2 inches (5 cm) from apex on all lines, also notch apex.
5. Draw a ⅛ inch (3 mm) curve down both dart legs starting at bottom control notch and ending at waist. **Note: This will add shape to the bodice under the bust.**
6. Close side dart using slash-and-spread method
7. Cut curved slash line to the edge of the dart point.
8. Cut dart leg to the edge of the dart point.
9. Close dart and tape shut.
10. Straighten side-seam if not straight.
11. Cut front and side-front pieces apart, making sure to cut out the darts.
12. Mark grain line for side-front pattern perpendicular to waistline.
13. Smooth out the bust line and front princess line if they look too pointy or uneven.
14. Walk the pattern from the waist up and waist down using an awl, adjusting pattern and notches as needed to balance style line at armhole and hemline. **Note: Retain the notches on the side-front piece and adjust the front pattern notches when walking the seam.**

AUTHOR TIP

Note: As a rule, you should place control notches every 15 inches (37.5 cm) to ensure sewing accuracy.

Back princess style line

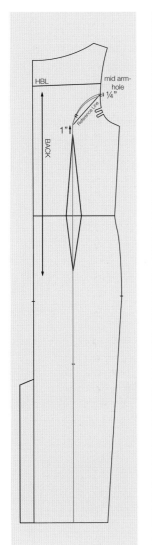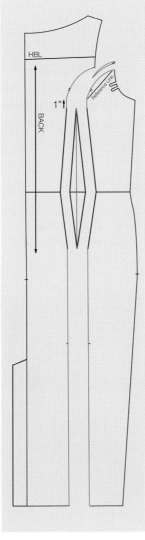

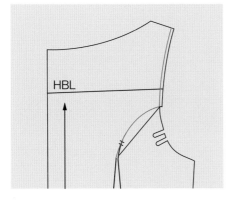

1. For the back block, extend the contour dart center line (red line) up 1 inch (2.5 cm) from top dart point and continue down to hem.
2. Mark a control notch midway between waist and hem.
3. Draw a straight line from the extended center line of the dart point to mid-armhole (this gives you a reference point for the princess line). **Note: You can mark this point wherever you like, but remember, the closer to the underarm, the more curved the princess line will be.**
4. Draw a curved line from armhole to dart point (red line); double notch for back.
5. Draw another curved line ¼ inch (6 mm) down from princess line, connecting with the original curve equal to the length of the original back shoulder dart.
6. Mark grain line for side-back pattern perpendicular to waistline.
7. Cut out back and side-back patterns, making sure to eliminate the darts.
8. Smooth out princess style line if necessary.
9. Walk the pattern from the waist up and the waist down using an awl, adjusting the pattern as needed to balance style line at armhole and hemline.

Bandeau collar

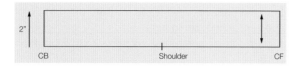

1. For collar, draw a horizontal line equal to the front and back neckline measurement.
2. Mark CB and CF.
3. Using back neckline measurement, mark shoulder and notch.
4. Square a line 2 inches (5 cm) up from CF and CB and connect.
5. Mark grain line parallel to CF.

Muslin or Toile Fitting

- Before you draft the lining patterns, prepare a muslin for fit.
- Do not add seam allowance (SA) to pattern, as you will most likely be adjusting the muslin for fit.
- Draw the SA directly on to the muslin after tracing the working pattern.
- Make any necessary fit corrections to pattern.
- Now you can move on to the lining patterns.

> **AUTHOR TIP**
>
> Note: You can either sew or pin muslin. I prefer to pin, as you can make quick adjustments to the fit of the garment on the dress form.

Figure 2.8
Checking muslin for fit.

Figure 2.9
Close-up of muslin neckline.

Completing the bandeau collar

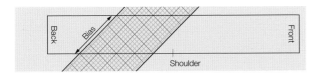

1. Fold paper in half and trace the collar to mirror the top neckline pattern piece; don't forget to mark your shoulder notch.
2. Cut out pattern piece while paper is still folded.
3. Mark fold line on the pattern.
   Note: As this is a straight collar, you can combine the upper and under collars together.

Armhole bias binding

1. For bias binding draw a horizontal line equal to front and back armhole measurement.
2. Mark shoulder seam and notch.
3. Square a line 2 inches (5 cm) from both ends of line and connect to make a rectangle.
4. Mark the grain line on the bias by placing the ruler at a 90-degree angle.
   Note: Depending on the weight of your fabric, you can choose to sew a single bias or French bias binding.

Front, side-front, and side-back lining

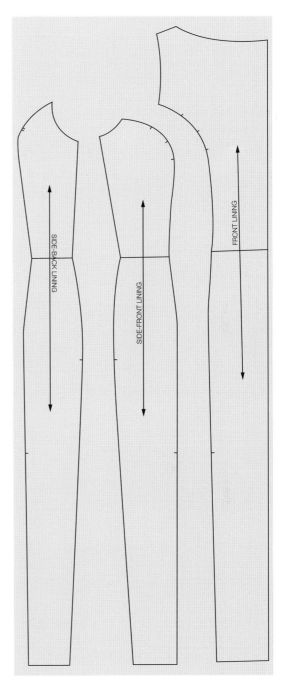

1. Trace front, side-front, and side-back pattern pieces; label them as shown, and set aside.

Left and right back lining

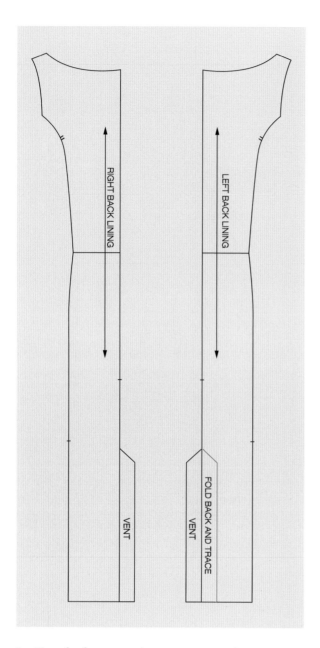

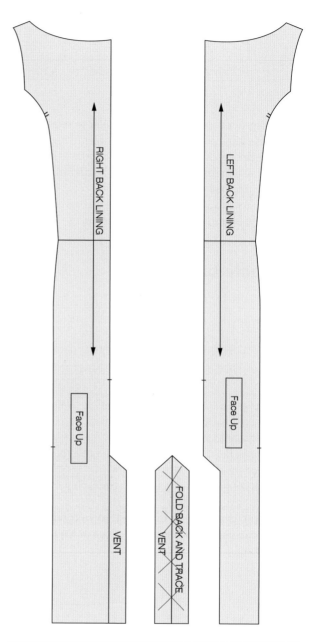

1. Trace back pattern piece, turn over, and trace again.
2. Right back pattern piece remains the same.
3. For left back lining, fold pattern back at vent fold line and trace.
4. Cut out vent piece and discard as shown.
5. Write "face-up" on both pattern pieces.

AUTHOR TIP

Lining patterns are reversed, as they are "inside out" from the self-pattern pieces, so take care when sewing the lining together so the back-vent opening is correct.

Production Pattern

Seam allowances and hems

Front, back, side-front, and side-back seam allowances and hems

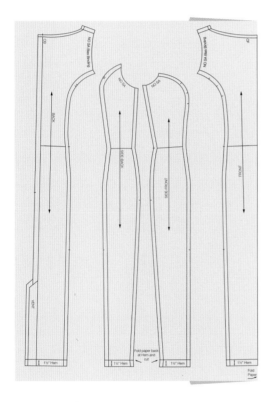

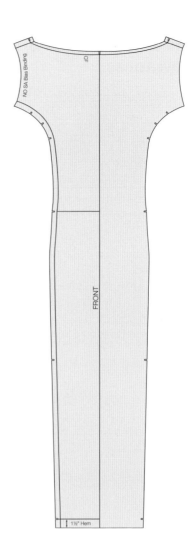

6. Add ¼ inch (6 mm) SA to neckline seams and length of back vent, as shown.
7. Do not add SA to armholes, as they are bias bound. **Note: For front pattern piece, mark SAs and cut out pattern while paper is still folded!**
8. Circle and drill back-vent stitching stop point ⅛ inch (3mm) into the SA, as shown.
9. The hem is 1½ inches (3.75 cm), so notch this.

1. Mirror front pattern piece.
2. Fold pattern paper in half and trace front pattern piece.
3. Trace side-front, side-back, and back pattern pieces.
4. Add ½ inch (1.2 cm) SA to princess lines, side-seam pieces, and slanted line of back vent, as shown.
5. Add 1 inch (2.5 cm) SA to back seam for lapped zipper. **Note: If you are not sewing a lapped zipper, the back SA will be ½ inch (1.2 cm).**

Collar and armhole bias binding seam allowances

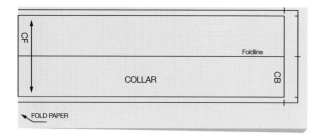

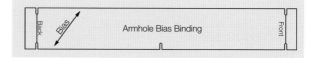

1. Fold paper in half and trace collar to mirror the CF of the pattern piece.
2. Add ¼ inch (6 mm) SA to neckline seams.
3. Add 1 inch SA (2.5 cm) to CB seams (for lapped zipper application).
4. Mark grain lines parallel to fold line on collar, as shown.

5. Notch fold line.
   Note: Mark SAs and cut out pattern while paper is still folded!
6. For armhole bias binding, add ½ inch SA (1.2 cm) at the front and back underarm seams, as shown.

Front, back, side-front, and side-back lining seam allowances and hems

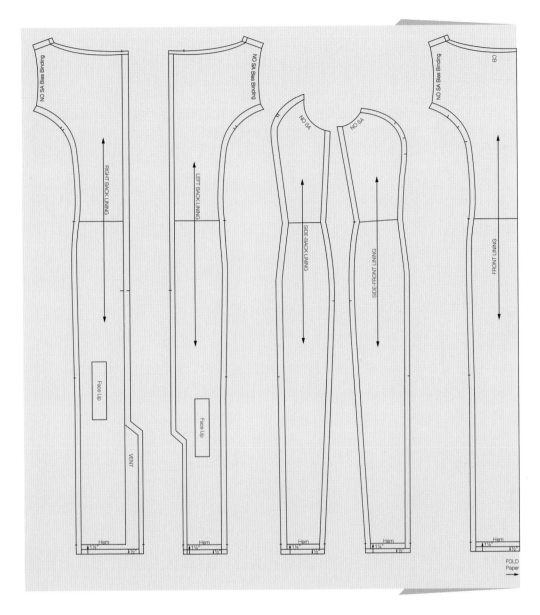

1. Mirror front lining pattern piece.
2. Fold pattern paper in half and trace front pattern piece.
3. Trace side-front, side-back, and both back pattern pieces.
4. Add ½ inch (1.2 cm) SA to princess lines and side-seam pieces and slanted line of back vent, as shown.
5. Add 1 inch (2.5 cm) SA to back seam for lapped zipper.
6. Add ¼ inch (6 mm) SA to neckline seams and length of back vent, as shown.
7. Do not add SA to armholes, as they are bias bound.**Note: For front pattern piece, mark SAs and cut out pattern while paper is still folded!**
8. Extend lining hem ½ inch (1.2 cm) on all pattern pieces.
9. Notch hem 1¼ inches (3 cm) up into the pattern. This will allow the lining to hang ¾ inch (1.75 cm) above skirt hem on the finished garment.

TECHNICAL FLATS AND FINISHED PATTERN PIECES

Technical flat front

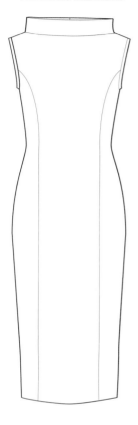

Technical flat back

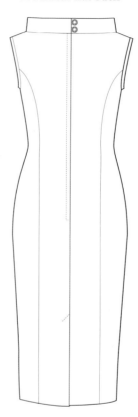

Self

1. Front (cut 1).
2. Side-front (cut 2).
3. Back (cut 2).
4. Side-back (cut 2).
5. Bandeau collar (cut 2).
6. Armhole bias binding (cut 2).

Lining

1. Front (cut 1).
2. Side-front (cut 2).
3. Left back (cut 1).
4. Right back (cut 1).
5. Side-back (cut 2).

"Style is knowing who you are, what you want to say, and not giving a damn."

Orson Welles

Figure 2.10
Back neckline detail.

The Shift Dress

Patterning concepts learned

- Relaxed fit
- Modified three-quarter set-in sleeve
- Funnel/stovepipe neckline
- Bust dart released into seam
- Inverted pleat
- Neckline facing
- Lining patterns

Figure 3.1
Designed shift dress.

The History of the Shift Dress

The shift dress is most associated with the 1960s' "youth quake" movement in London and the United States. In actuality, the cut of the shift dress with its unfitted waistline and hip-skimming skirt was first favored by flappers in the roaring twenties because it was comfortable and easy to dance in. The term "flapper" is said to have originated in the jazz clubs and speakeasies these women frequented: while dancing the Charleston, their arms and feet moved so rapidly that they resembled birds flapping their wings. A departure from the cinched waist and long skirts of the time, the shift was also associated with artists and the suffragette movement during this period. While Jeanne Lanvin is credited with creating the modern-day chemise dress in the early 1920s, it was Paul Poiret who, as early as 1900, created dresses that de-emphasized curves in favor of a sleek look, freeing women at last from the corset. Both the chemise and shift dresses have a similar silhouette, and they additionally share a history of outfitting the unconventional women of the day, who wore these styles to set themselves apart from mainstream society in their choice of dress and attitude.

In the mid-1950s the structured silhouette that had dominated the post-war years got a fresh take when

Cristóbal Balenciaga reintroduced the unfitted style line and Christian Dior introduced his A-line collection. But both looks had minimal success, and critics of the style dubbed it a "sack." It was not until the Mods, a youth movement in 1960s' London, adopted the look as their own that the shift became a fashion mainstay. Breaking from the fashions of their parents, they "shifted" the lines between generations. They wanted to separate

Figure 3.3
Fashion designer Mary Quant wearing a mini-dress of her own design, 1966.

Figure 3.2
American actress, dancer, and flapper Violet Romer in flapper dress, c. 1910–1915.

themselves from the norm, and used their mode of dress to help define the look of a new generation. Their version of the shift was anything but soft, integrating a harder and more geometric line.

During this period the boutique Biba on Kensington High Street and fashion designer Mary Quant's shop Bazaar played a pivotal role in the shift's endearing style.

Quant opened Bazaar in London's Chelsea neighborhood in 1955. The shop offered affordable clothing that catered to her contemporaries, and was an instant success. Dissatisfied with the merchandise she could find wholesale, Quant started stocking the store with designs of her own, which became an instant sensation amongst her peers. Self-taught, she would sew up new creations every night to stock the store, which would promptly sell out. The shift was a mainstay in the shop, and her customers kept coming back for shorter versions of the popular dress. Quant not only designed but also lived the lifestyle, and her look became the quintessential "Chelsea girl" style. By the mid-1960s the unfitted style of the shift was almost universally worn.

The boutique Biba also offered up-to-the-minute styles that were hip and affordable to the younger generation. In 1963 Barbara Hulanicki, with the help of her husband, launched Biba's Postal Boutique as a mail-order business. A year later her pink-gingham sleeveless shift dress was featured in an article on women in business in the UK newspaper the *Daily Mirror*. The fresh, simple silhouette of the dress was so appealing that a remarkable 17,000 orders were placed, giving Hulanicki the courage to open her first store. Once again, the affordability of the designs kept people coming back for more.

Young French fashion designers such as Yves Saint Laurent, Pierre Cardin, and André Courrèges also contributed to the shift's global success. The 1960s were a time of change, and these young designers wanted to appeal to the younger generation. They expanded their houses to sell versions of their couture pieces as "prêt-à-porter" or "ready-to-wear," and were able to offer their futuristic looks to the masses. But while the French houses helped to cement the shift's global appeal, it was the lifestyle of the Mods on the scene that made the look affordable and fresh to a whole generation.

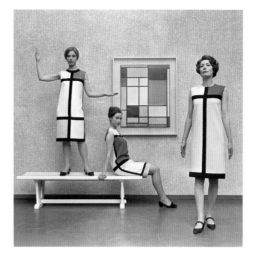

Figure 3.4
Models wearing shift dresses designed by Yves Saint Laurent and inspired by Mondrian paintings, 1966.

Figure 3.5
A woman wearing a shift dress talks to a man wearing full leopard print outfit in New York City, The LIFE Picture Collection, 1969.

"The fashionable woman wears clothes; the clothes don't wear her."

Mary Quant

Contemporary Shifts

Whether an homage to the 1960s' silhouette or a completely fresh take, the modern shift's no-nonsense appeal speaks to its modern audience.

Figure 3.6
Courrèges, Runway, Paris Fashion Week, Fall/Winter 2019/2020.

Figure 3.7
Yohji Yamamoto, Runway, Paris Fashion Week, Spring/Summer 2020.

The Pattern

Start with torso front, back, and
sleeve blocks

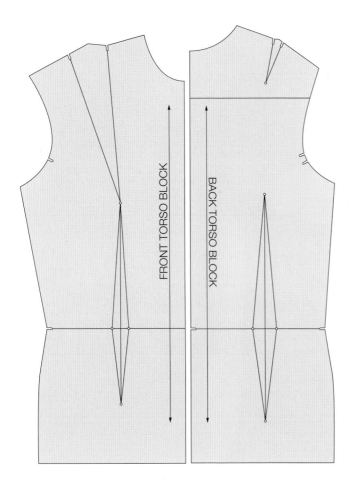

FRONT TORSO BLOCK

BACK TORSO BLOCK

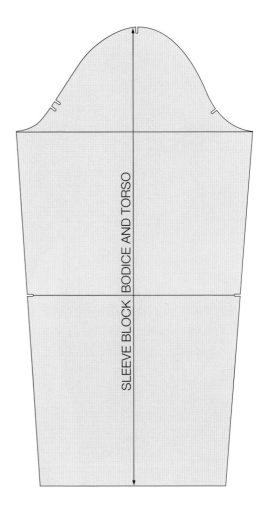

SLEEVE BLOCK BODICE AND TORSO

Front, back, and sleeve development

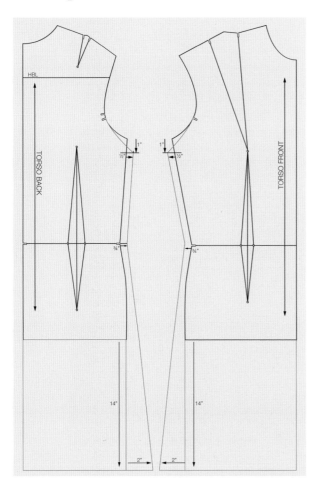

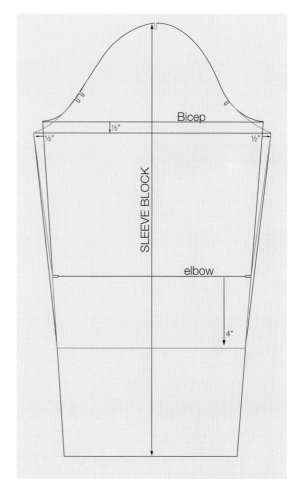

1. Trace the front and back patterns.
2. Extend length 14 inches (35 cm). **Note: You can extend the length as much or as little as you prefer.**
3. Lower armscye 1 inch (2.5 cm).
4. Mark out ½ inch (1.2 cm) out from underarm, ¾ inch (1.75 cm) at waistline, and 2 inches (5 cm) out at hem, and draw new side-seams. **Note: These measurements can be adjusted for desired fit and flare of the skirt.**
5. True up armhole curve with French curve, making sure the front armhole measurement is ½ inch (1.2 cm) smaller than the back armhole measurement.

1. Trace sleeve block. Draw a parallel line ½ inch (1.2 cm) below bicep line and extend ½ inch (1.2 cm) out from armhole. **Note: The amount the torso is widened and the armscye lowered can be adjusted as desired for fit—just make sure when you lower the armhole and bicep that the proportions are in a 2:1 ratio.**
2. Draw new armhole with French curve blending to new bicep line and underarm seam, making sure the extended measurements for the front and back dress armholes equal the extended measurements for the sleeve. This will guarantee that the set-in sleeve still retains its ease.
3. For a three-quarter sleeve, mark 4 inches (10 cm) below elbow and draw a parallel line.
4. Draw a straight line for underarm seam and then curve slightly for closer fit.

Releasing front bust dart into seam and front inverted pleat

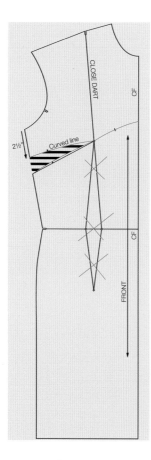

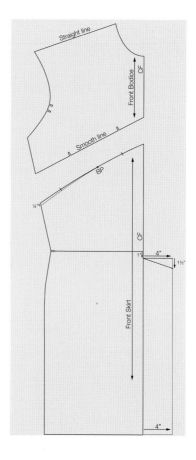

1. Draw a curved line from the side-seam, starting 2½ inches (6.2 cm) below armhole and passing through the apex (bust point) to the center front (CF). **Note: This can be any shape you want as long as the line passes through the apex.**
2. Notch pattern as shown on curved line.
3. Transfer shoulder dart to side-seam by the slash-and-spread method
4. Cut slash line from this curved line to the apex (bust point).
5. Cut another slash line down the dart leg on shoulder.
6. Close shoulder dart and tape shut.
7. Straighten shoulder line if not straight.
8. Release contour dart (red Xs). **Note: Releasing a dart simply means to ignore it.**

9. Cut pattern apart on curved line, retaining bust point on bottom pattern.
10. To prevent the side-seam from pitching forward, you must adjust the dart intake on the side-seam. On bottom pattern, mark ¼ inch (6 mm) down on side-seam and blend to apex.
11. Smooth curved lines on patterns as needed. **Note: This measurement may need to be adjusted depending on the bust size. Keep adjusting the measurement until the side-seam is perpendicular on the muslin or toile.**
12. For an inverted pleat, extend a parallel line 2½ inches (6.2 cm) down and 4 inches (10 cm) out from CF.
13. Mark 1 inch (2.5 cm) down on CF and draw a slanted line to complete the inverted pleat, as shown.
14. Retain waist and hip notches on side-seam.
15. Label front bodice and front skirt.

Separating back pieces

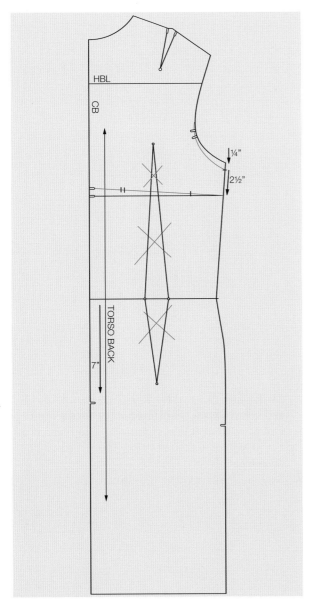

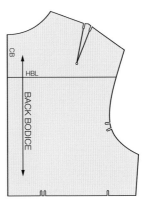

1. Release back contour darts (red Xs).
2. Measure 7 inches (17.5 cm) down from center back (CB) waist and notch for zipper placement. Retain waist and hip notches on the side-seam.
3. Lower back armhole ¼ inch (6 mm) and blend armscye with French ruler. (This equals the measurement of the front dart intake.)
4. Square a line 2½ inches (6.2 cm) down from new armhole to CB, and then curve to desired shape.
5. Notch as shown and cut pattern pieces apart. Make sure that one of the notches is a double notch as it is a back pattern piece.
6. Label back bodice and back skirt.

Front funnel neckline

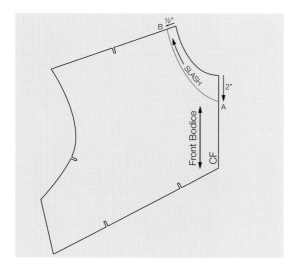

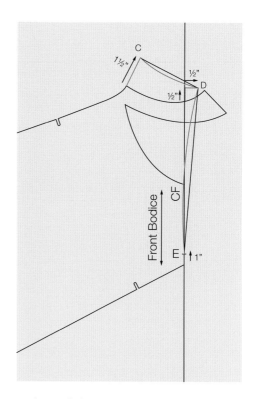

1. Mark the back shoulder dart placement on the front pattern.
2. For top front bodice pattern, draw a curved line ½ inch (1.2 cm) in from high-point shoulder and 2 inches (5 cm) down from CF neckline. Label A and B, as shown.

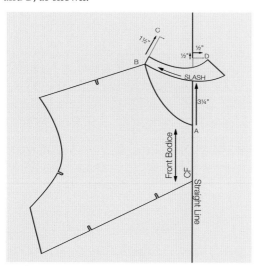

7. Mark 1 inch (2.5 cm) up from CF as shown, label E, and notch. This is your stitching line for the front.
8. Draw two straight lines connecting C to D and D to E. Curve lines to desired shape. This is the neckline opening.
9. Smooth shoulder curve as shown.

3. Cut the curved line from point A to point B by the slash-and-spread method.
4. Draw a straight line on a piece of paper, securing the bottom CF to it. Spread the top CF piece 3¼ inches (8 cm) and secure.
5. Extend shoulder line 1½ inches (3.75 cm) at high-point shoulder, label C, and square out as shown.
6. Extend CF line up ½ inch (1.2 cm) from original neckline curve and square out ½ inch (1.2cm); label D.

Back funnel neckline

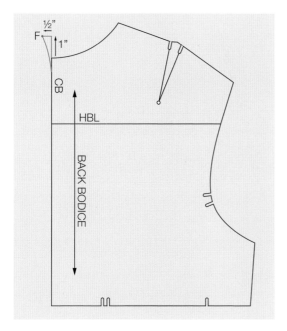

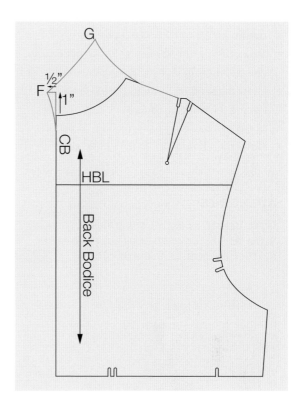

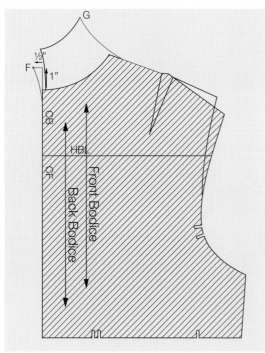

1. For back bodice, extend CB neckline up 1 inch (2.5 cm).
2. Square a short line out ½ inch (1.2 cm) and label F.
3. Draw a curved line from CB neckline to F, as shown.
4. Place front bodice on top of back bodice, lining up at the shoulder seams; make sure to match front shoulder notch with back dart placement.
5. Trace front shoulder/neckline on to back bodice pattern as shown, squaring off at neckline, and label G.
6. Connect F to G with a slightly curved line.
7. Label back bodice.

Muslin or Toile Fitting

- Before you draft the lining patterns, prepare a muslin for fit.
- Do not add seam allowance (SA) to pattern, as you will most likely be adjusting the muslin for fit.
- Draw the SA directly on to the muslin after tracing the working pattern.
- Make any necessary fit corrections to pattern.
- Now you can move on to the lining patterns.

> **AUTHOR TIP**
>
> Note: You can either sew or pin muslin. I prefer to pin, as you can make quick adjustments to the fit of the garment on the dress form.

Figure 3.8
Muslin fit with sleeve added.

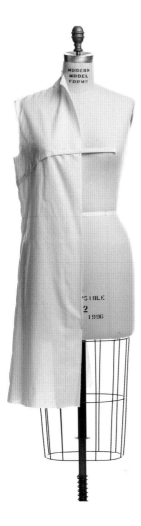

Figure 3.9
Checking muslin fit before sleeve is added.

Front facing and front bodice lining

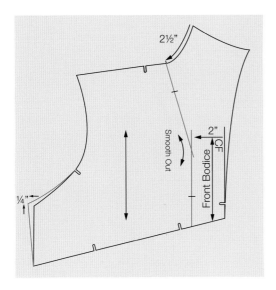

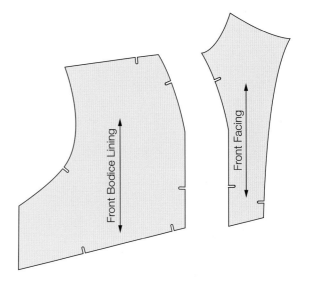

1. Trace front bodice pattern.
2. Draw a parallel line 2 inches (5 cm) from CF.
3. Square a line 2½ inches (6 cm) from neckline edge until both lines intersect.
4. Smooth out where the lines intersect.

5. Mark two control notches for sewing guide, as shown.
6. Starting at the bottom of the side-seam, draw a line out and up ¼ inch (6 mm) to allow for ease in the lining pattern.
7. Blend to front armhole notch.
8. Mark grain lines parallel to CF.
9. Cut apart and label front facing and front bodice lining.

Back facing and back bodice lining

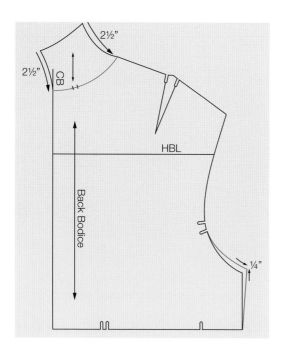

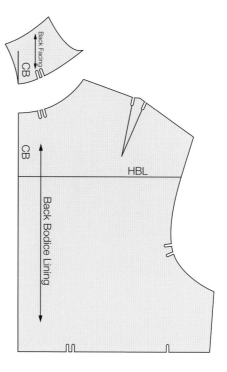

1. Trace back bodice pattern.
2. For back facing, draw a curved line 2½ inches (6 cm) from neckline and notch as shown.
3. Starting at the bottom of the side-seam, draw a line out and up ¼ inch (6 mm) to allow for ease in the lining pattern.

4. Blend to back armhole notch.
5. Mark grain lines parallel to CB.
6. Cut apart and label back facing and back bodice lining.

Sleeve lining

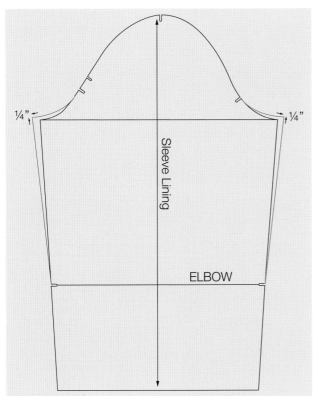

1. Trace sleeve pattern.
2. Starting at the elbow, draw out and up ¼ inch (6 mm) to allow for ease in the lining pieces.
3. Blend armhole curves to notches.
4. Label sleeve lining.

Front skirt lining and inverted pleat facing

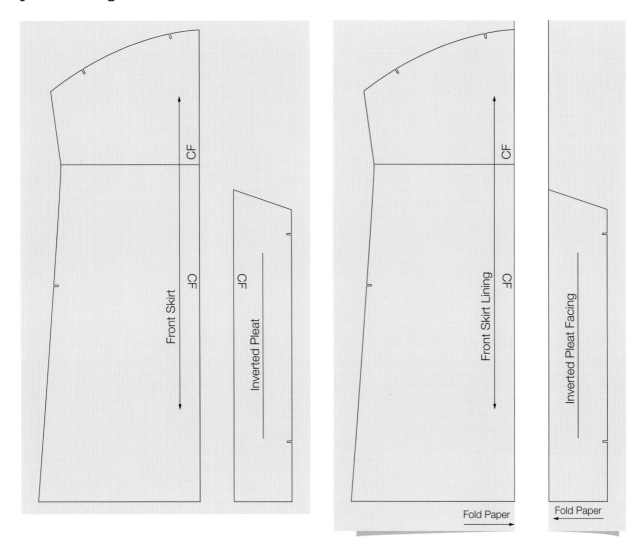

1. Trace front skirt pattern, notch along the edge of the inverted pleat as shown, and cut out, dividing the skirt and inverted pleat at CF into two pieces. Make sure to transfer the new notches to the original pattern.
2. Fold paper in half and trace the front skirt inverted pleat patterns, aligning the CF with the fold.

3. Mark grain lines parallel to CF.
4. Label front skirt lining and inverted pleat facing, and set aside.

Back skirt lining

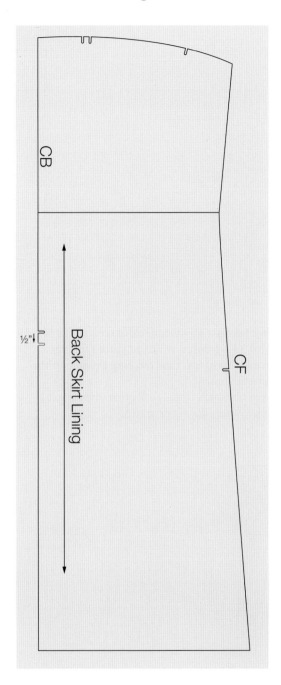

CB

Back Skirt Lining

CF

½"↓

Production Pattern
Seam allowances and hems

1. Trace back skirt pattern.
2. Lower CB zipper notch by ½ inch (1.2 cm).
3. Label back skirt lining. **Note: Do not cut pattern pieces out until SA has been added.**

Front bodice, back bodice, and sleeve seam allowances and hems

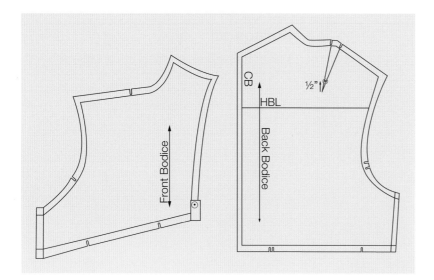

1. Add ½ inch (1.2 cm) SA to all seams with the exception of the front and back necklines and the CF seam.
2. Add ¼ inch (6 mm) SA to the front and back necklines and the CF seam, stopping at the notch.
3. Add ½ inch (1.2 cm) SA to the remaining portion of the CF seam. **Note: The CF seam allowances change because an open neckline requires a ¼ inch (6 mm) SA while a sewn front seam requires a ½ inch (1.2 cm) SA, thus creating the step in the pattern as shown.**
4. Replace CF notch with a drill point, marking it ⅛ inch (3 mm) down and into SA.

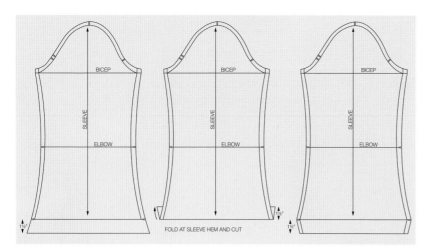

5. Circle and drill back shoulder dart point ½ inch (1.2 cm) into the dart.
6. Mark sleeve hem 1½ inches (3.75 cm). This includes the ½ inch (1.2 cm) SA.

AUTHOR TIP

Make sure to fold paper back at hemline when cutting out sleeve to ensure the hem lies correctly on the garment.

Front skirt, back skirt, and inverted pleat facing seam allowances and hems

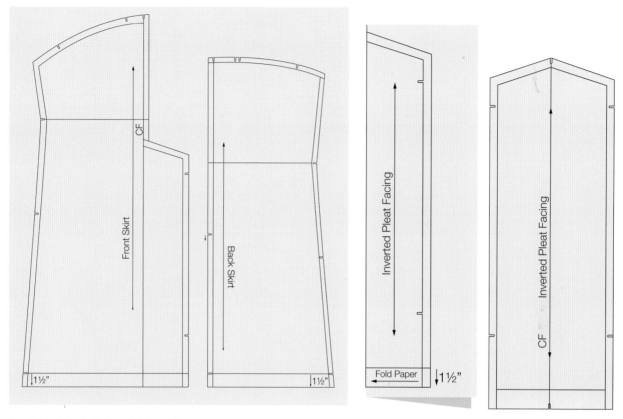

1. Add ½ inch (1.2 cm) SA to all seams.
2. Mark hems at 1½ inches (3.75 cm). **Note: For inverted pleat facing, mark SA, hem, and notches while paper is still folded and cut out.**
3. Notch CF at hem.

Front and back facings seam allowances

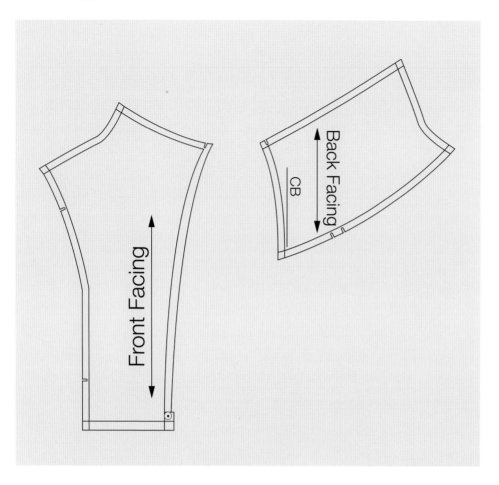

1. Add ½ inch (1.2 cm) SA to all seams with the exception of the front and back necklines and the CF seam.
2. Add ¼ inch (6 mm) SA to the front and back necklines and down the CF seam, stopping at the notch.
3. Add ½ inch (1.2 cm) SA to the remaining portion of the CF seam.
4. Replace CF notch with a drill point, marking it ⅛ inch (3 mm) down and into SA.

Front bodice lining, back bodice lining, front skirt lining, back skirt lining, and sleeve lining seam allowances and hems

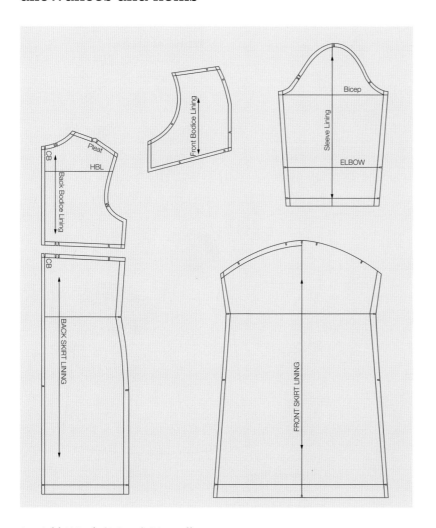

1. Add ½ inch (1.2 cm) SA to all seams.
2. Turn back shoulder dart into a pleat, retaining dart notches.
3. For the front and back skirt lining hem, do not add any SA; simply notch the pattern 1 inch (2.5 cm) up. **Note: For front skirt lining, mark SA, hem, and notches while paper is still folded and cut out.**
4. For the sleeve hem, do not add any SA; simply notch the pattern ½ inch (1.2 cm) up.

AUTHOR TIP

When marking a hem for lining, the hem generally matches the fold-line for the finished hem on the self-pattern regardless of the size of the hem.

TECHNICAL FLATS AND FINISHED PATTERN PIECES

Technical flat front

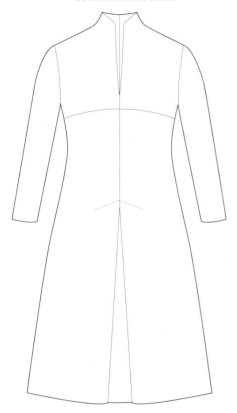

Technical flat back

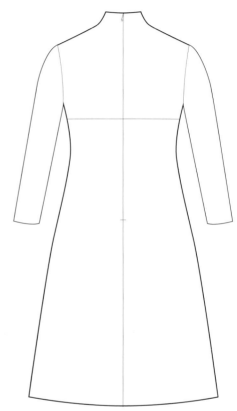

Self
Front bodice (cut 2)
Back bodice (cut 2)
Sleeve (cut 2)
Front facing (cut 2)
Back facing (cut 2)

Contrast
Front skirt (cut 2)
Back skirt (cut 2)
Inverted pleat facing (cut 1)

Interfacing
Front facing (cut 2)
Back facing (2)

Lining
Front bodice (cut 2)
Back bodice (cut 2)
Sleeve (cut 2)
Front skirt (cut 1)
Back skirt (cut 2)

"Fashion wasn't what you wore someplace anymore; it was the whole reason for going."

Andy Warhol

Figure 3.10
Front neckline detail.

The Trapeze Dress

Patterning concepts learned

- Trapeze style line
- Transferring darts to hemline
- Neckline contouring
- Adding volume to style lines
- All-in-one facing
- Lining patterns

Figure 4.1
Designed trapeze dress.

The History of the Trapeze Dress

Deceptively simple to the eye, the original trapeze collection designed by Yves Saint Laurent for Dior in 1958 was anything but simple. This style, derived from Dior's A-line dress, flared from a fitted bust to create a trapezoid shape. Its inner structure consisted of a close-fitting lining that enabled the dress to be fitted through the front bodice but also flare from the back shoulder line. Laurent, 21 at the time, was the youngest couturier in the world, and conveyed his youthful point of view regarding the future of fashion in a press release stating that "the figure was lost in favor of style." The same year, designers Cristóbal Balenciaga and Hubert de Givenchy introduced their own version of the overly dramatic A-line, which came to be known as the "baby-doll" dress.

This change of silhouette can be interpreted as the foundation for the emerging fashion divide between generations, where the youth culture of the 1960s clashed with convention. But in 1958 Paris, with all its decorum, still dictated the fashions of the day. Stylish women had no choice but to conform or risk being considered a social outcast in polite society. The term "slave to fashion" had a serious place in sartorial history at this time, when strict rules about something as mundane as hem lengths were followed with exact precision. The revolutionary shape of the trapeze was adopted for just a few seasons by very fashionable women, but never gained a stronghold in the emerging ready-to-wear market at the time. For most, it was too radical a shift in silhouette to catch on, and it didn't become a fashion staple until a more subtle, shorter, and fitted version of the A-line was introduced in the 1960s.

Throughout the 1960s and into the 1970s the A-line silhouette embodied the liberation and social values of the women who wore it. Givenchy, who was known for his sculptural forms, said at the time "I've dreamt of a liberated woman who will no longer be swathed in fabric, armour-plated. All my lines are styles for quick and fluid movement." The A-line is a simplified version of the trapeze, and much more flattering. A proper A-line dress is a structured garment that is fitted through the shoulders and gradually flares away from the body to the hem, resembling its namesake letter A. Young designers and their female followers embraced the silhouette and quickly adopted it in their wardrobes, making it shorter and shorter. The shape embodied a fresh new approach to fashion—one of youth and rebellion.

The trapeze line has remained a constant source of inspiration for designers over the years. Known for their *avant garde* aesthetic and unconventional silhouettes, Japanese designers such as Issey Miyake, Yohji Yamamoto, and Rei Kawakubo of Comme des Garçons consistently show versions of the silhouette in their collections. Mainstream designers of late are also getting in on the action, and the trapeze line is enjoying a renaissance today.

Figure 4.2
A model poses for the first Yves Saint Laurent Dior collection, when he introduced the trapeze dress in 1958.

Figure 4.3
Philadelphia Museum of Art 2018 Fabulous Fashion Exhibition of designer Cristóbal Balenciaga's "baby-doll dress", 1957.

Figure 4.4
Model wearing a design from Jacques Esterel's Spring/ Summer Collection, 1967.

Figure 4.5
English model Twiggy sits cross-legged in an exotic tent constructed in Justin de Villeneuve's home, early 1970s.

"Over the years I have learned that what is important in a dress is the woman who's wearing it."

Yves Saint Laurent

Contemporary Trapeze Dresses

A timeless shape gets modernized.

Figure 4.6
Lanvin, Runway, Paris Fashion Week, Fall/ Winter 2020/2021.

Figure 4.7
Gareth Pugh, Runway, London Fashion Week, September 2016.

The Pattern

Start with front torso contour and back torso blocks

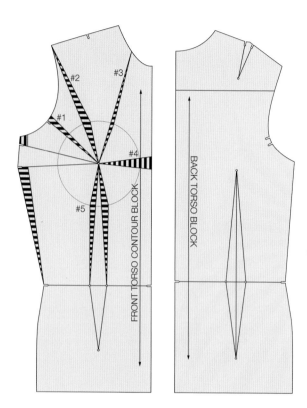

Lengthen pattern and release contour waist darts

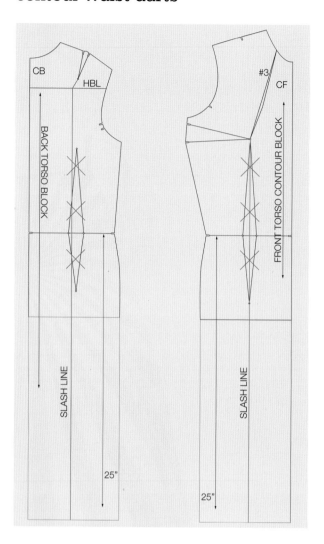

1. Trace front and back patterns.
2. Transfer contour guideline 3 to the front pattern.
3. Lengthen torso 25 inches (62.5 cm) from waist.
   Note: You can extend the length as much or as little as you prefer.
4. Release contour waist darts on both front and back patterns (red Xs). **Note: Releasing a dart simply means to ignore it.**
5. Extend back shoulder dart leg to the horizontal balance line (HBL) and square a slash line (red line) to the hemline. **Note: The slash line may not pass through the center of the dart.**
6. On the front pattern, draw a slash line (red line) from the bust point (apex) parallel to the center front (CF) to the hemline.

Transferring back shoulder dart to hemline and side-seam development

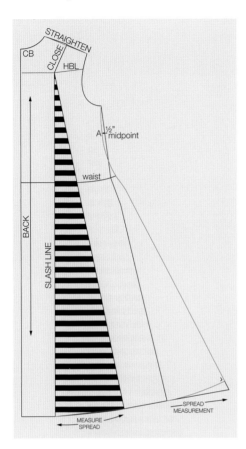

Back neckline development

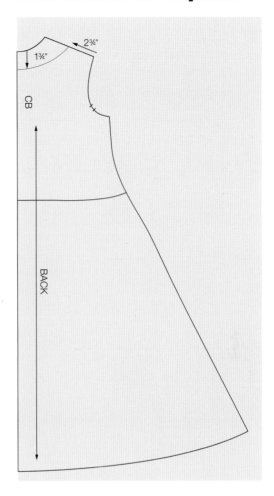

1. Transfer back shoulder dart to hemline using the slash-and-spread method.
2. Cut shoulder dart leg to the edge of the HBL.
3. Cut slash line to the edge of the HBL.
4. Close shoulder dart and tape shut.
5. Straighten shoulder seam (red line) if necessary.
6. Measure the dart spread and record_____.
7. Add the dart spread measurement to the side-seam.
8. Measure back hemline sweep and record_____.
9. For side-seam development, measure and mark the midpoint of the armhole to the waist.
10. Measure in ½ inch (1.2 cm) from the midpoint and label A.
11. Draw a curved line (red line) from the armhole passing through A and blending to the hemline.
12. Adjust the length of the side-seam to equal original waist-to-hem measurement of 25 inches (62.5 cm).
13. Square off side-seam and blend to the hemline, as shown.

1. Lower back neckline 1¾ inches (4.25 cm).
2. Mark shoulder seam 2¾ inches (6.75 cm) in from shoulder.
3. Redraw neckline (red line) using a French curve.

Front neckline contouring and side-seam development

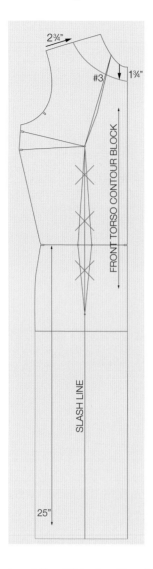

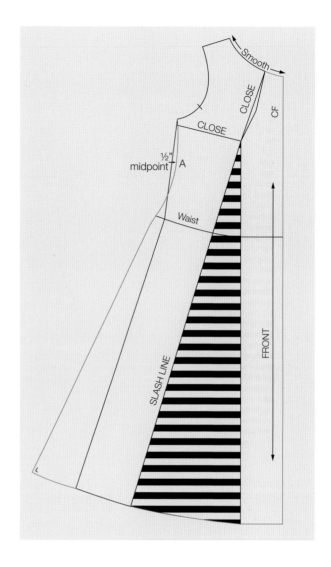

1. Lower front neckline 1¼ inches (3 cm).
2. Mark shoulder seam 2¾ inches (6.75 cm) in from shoulder.
3. Redraw neckline (red line) using a French curve.
4. Transfer contour guideline 3 and side-bust dart to hemline using the slash-and-spread method.
5. Cut both the side-bust dart and contour guideline 3 to the edge of the bust point (apex).
6. Cut the slash line to the edge of the bust point (apex).
7. Close both the side-bust dart and contour guideline 3 and tape shut. **Note: The guideline will not fully close.**
8. Smooth out the neckline (red line).
9. Measure the front hemline sweep.
10. Add the difference of the front and back hemline sweep to the side-seam to balance the front and back hemlines.
11. For side-seam development, measure and mark the midpoint of the armhole to the waist.
12. Measure in ½ inch (1.2 cm) from the midpoint and label A.
13. Draw a curved line (red line) from the armhole passing through A and blending to the hemline.
14. Adjust the length of the side-seam to equal original waist-to-hem measurement of 25 inches (62.5 cm).
15. Square off side-seam and blend to the hemline, as shown.

First Muslin or Toile Fitting

- Before you draft the rest of the pattern, prepare a quick muslin for fit and to make sure the side-seams are balanced.
- Do not add seam allowance (SA) to the pattern, as you will most likely be adjusting the muslin for fit.
- Draw the SA directly on to the muslin after tracing the working pattern.
- Make any necessary fit corrections to pattern.
- Now you can move on to adding style lines and volume to the trapeze dress.

AUTHOR TIP

Note: You can either sew or pin muslin. I chose to sew this muslin, as it gives a better fit for the flared skirt on the dress form. Make sure the side-seam is perpendicular to the floor and not pitching forward or backward.

Figure 4.9
Checking pitch of side-seam.

Figure 4.8
Checking first muslin fit.

Front and back trapeze patterns

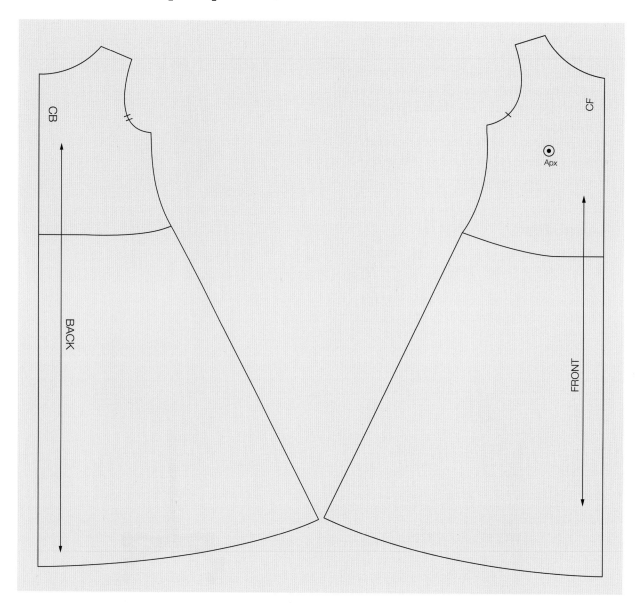

1. Trace both front and back trapeze patterns before you add style lines, and set aside for facing and lining development.

Side-front and side-back pattern style lines

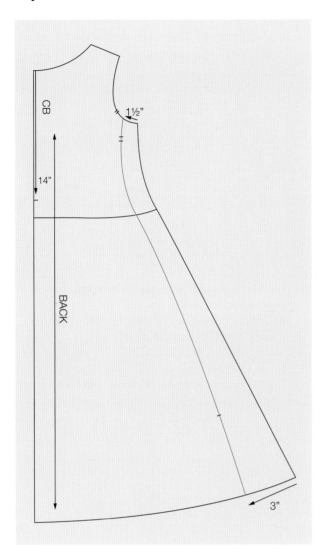

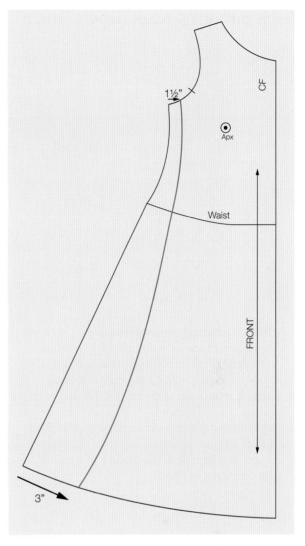

1. Trace front and back trapeze patterns.
2. Mark 14 inches (35 cm) down center back (CB) for zipper placement.
3. Mark in 1½ inches (3.75 cm) at armhole on both front and back patterns.
4. Mark 3 inches (7.5 cm) in at hemline on both front and back patterns.
5. Draw desired style line shape.

AUTHOR TIP

These style lines can be any shape you want. Try drawing on the muslin like a canvas to experiment with different shapes.

Back pattern pocket development

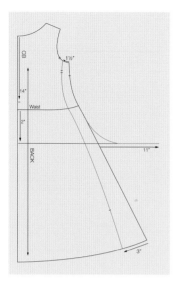 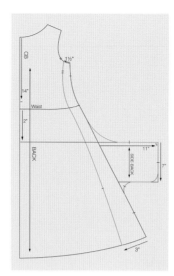 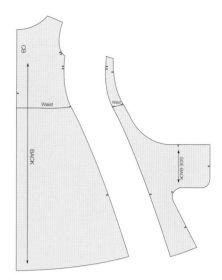

1. On back pattern, square a guideline for the top of the pocket 2 inches (5 cm) below CB waistline extending 11 inches (27.5 cm) from side-seam.
2. Draw a curved line (red line) from side-seam starting at the waist to the edge of the top pocket, as shown.
3. Square down 7 inches (17.5 cm) from edge of top pocket.
4. Square another line for the bottom of the pocket to the side-seam, as shown.
5. Connect top and bottom pocket, curving bottom edge of pocket.
6. Round out bottom pocket with French curve connecting it to side-seam, as shown.
7. Mark grain line parallel to CB.
8. Notch as shown.
9. Cut out pattern and label back and side-back.

Front pattern pocket development

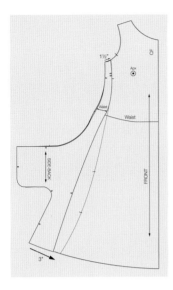 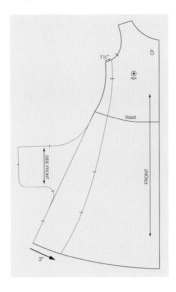 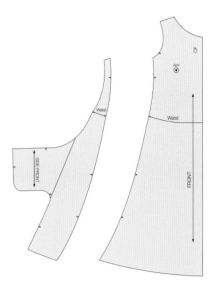

1. Place side-back pattern on front pattern matching at the side-seam waist notch and hemline.
2. Trace pocket shape on to front pattern, transferring notches.
3. Mark grain line parallel to CF.
4. Cut out patterns and label front and side-front.

Front and mid-front pattern

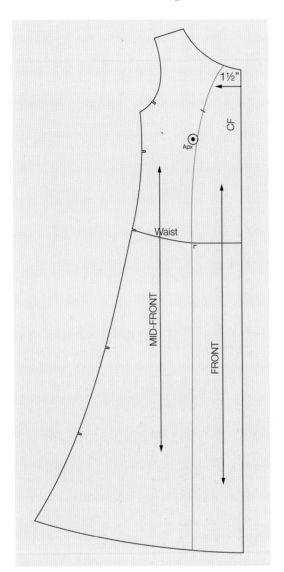

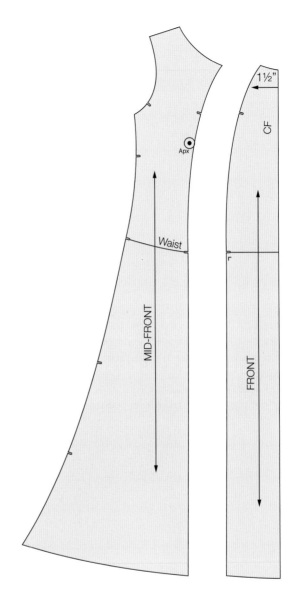

1. Mark 1½ inches (3.75 cm) in from CF at neckline.
2. Measure the distance from CF to bust point (apex), and mark this measurement on waist.
3. Draw desired shape from neckline to waist.
4. Square a guideline from waist down to hemline.
5. Mark grain lines parallel to CF and notch as shown.
6. Cut out patterns and label front and mid-front.

Adding volume to front and mid-front seams

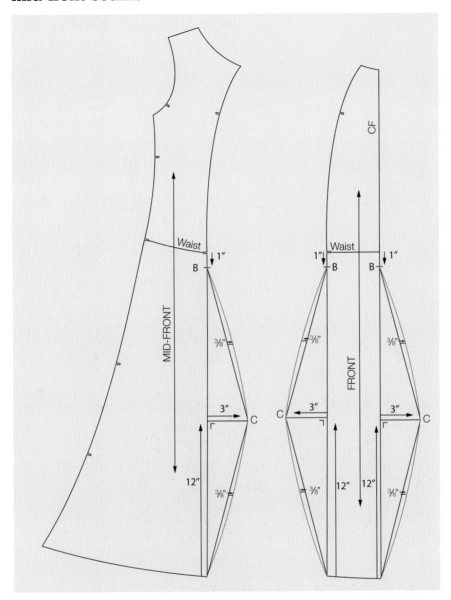

1. Trace front and mid-front pattern pieces, leaving room on the paper for the added volume.
2. Mark 1 inch (2.5 cm) below waist on patterns as shown; label B.
3. Mark 12 inches (30 cm) up from hemline and square 3 inches (7.5 cm) out; label C.
4. Draw straight guidelines connecting B to C and C to hemline.
5. Mark ⅜ inch (1 cm) out at midpoint of guidelines.
6. Draw curved lines (red lines) passing through all marks, making sure that all seams are identical.
7. Retain all notches and also notch at C.

Second Muslin or Toile Fitting

- Before you move on to facing and lining patterns, prepare a muslin for a second fitting.
- Do not add SA to pattern, as you will most likely be adjusting the muslin for fit.

- Draw the SA directly on to the muslin after tracing the working pattern.
- Make any necessary fit corrections to pattern.
- Now you can move on to the facing and lining patterns.

AUTHOR TIP

Note: You can either sew or pin muslin. I prefer to sew the second muslin, so you can access the added volume and style lines more accurately.

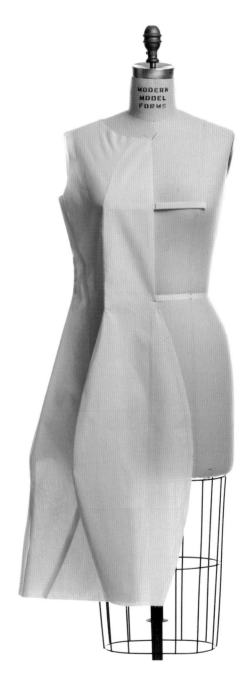

Figure 4.10
Checking second muslin fit.

Front and back facing and lining development

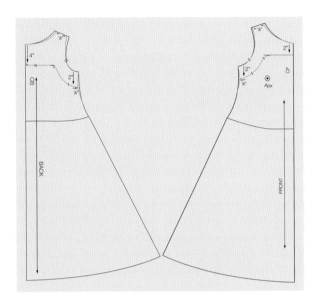
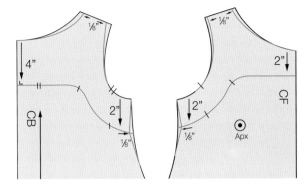

1. On the back trapeze pattern, square a line 4 inches (10 cm) down from CB and mark 2 inches (5 cm) around armhole until lines intersect.
2. On the front trapeze pattern, square a line 2 inches (5 cm) down from CF and mark 2 inches (5 cm) around armhole until lines intersect.
3. Smooth out the pointy parts, as shown, for both front and back facings.
4. Reduce the shoulder seams, necklines, and bottom edge of the side-seams by ⅛ inch (3 mm), as shown, blending to the original seams. **Note: You need to reduce the facing pieces so they roll into the inside of the garment when sewn.**
5. Notch as shown and cut apart.
6. Label front facing, back facing, front lining, and back lining.

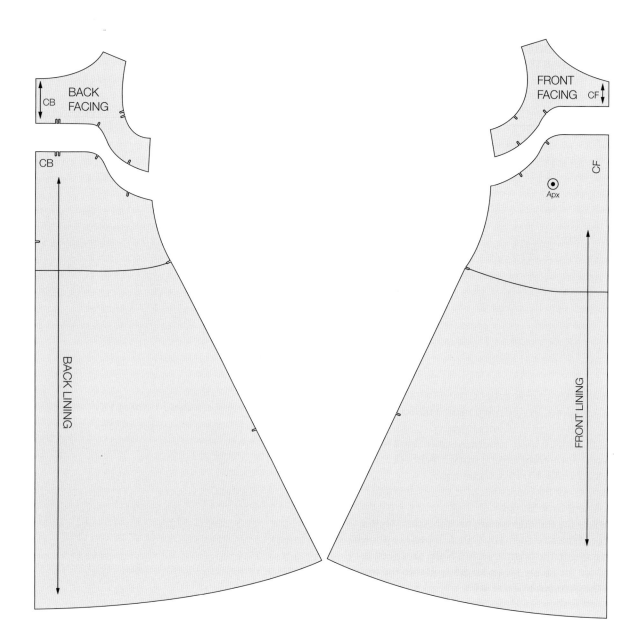

Production Pattern
Seam Allowances and Hems

Front, mid-front, side-front, back, and side-back seam allowances and hems

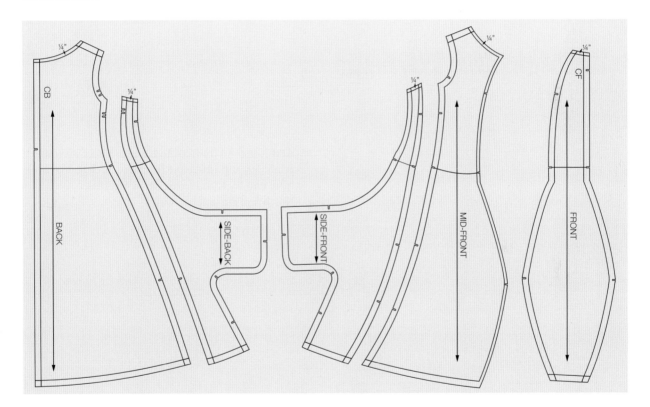

1. Add ½ inch (1.2 cm) SA to all seams with the exception of the necklines, armholes, and hems.
2. Add ¼ inch (6 mm) SA to the necklines, armholes, and hems.

Front and back facing seam allowances

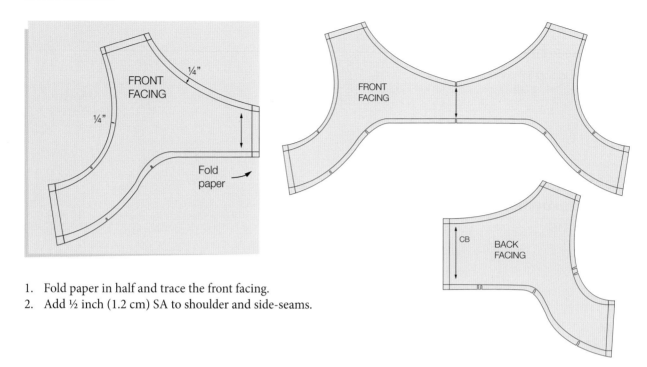

1. Fold paper in half and trace the front facing.
2. Add ½ inch (1.2 cm) SA to shoulder and side-seams.

3. Add ¼ inch (6 mm) SA to front and back necklines, armholes, and where the front and back facings and front and back linings are sewn together.
4. Notch and cut patterns out.

Front and back lining seam allowances and hems

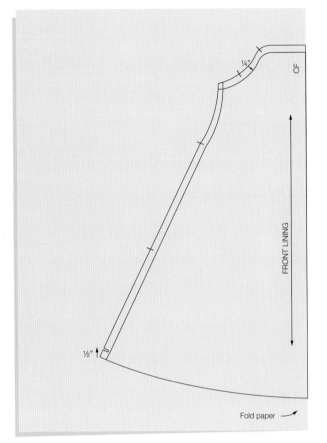

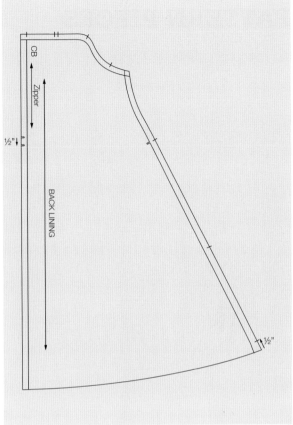

1. Fold paper in half and trace front lining pattern.
2. Trace back lining pattern.
3. Add 1/2 inch (1.2cm) SA to CB lining pattern and to side-seams on both front and back lining patterns.
4. Add 1/4 inch (6mm) SA to the top of the lining patterns.
5. You do not add a SA to the hem as it is already "built in," but mark 1/2 inch (1.2cm) up and notch.

TECHNICAL FLATS AND FINISHED PATTERN PIECES

Technical flat front

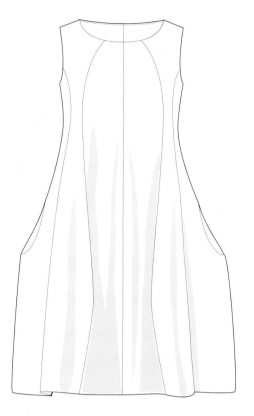

Technical flat back

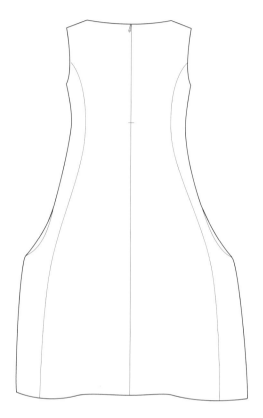

Self
Front (cut 2)
Mid-front (cut 2)
Side-front (cut 2)
Back (cut 2)
Side-back (cut 2)
Front facing (cut 1)
Back facing (cut 2)

Interfacing
Front facing (cut 1)
Back facing (cut 2)

Lining
Front lining (cut 1)
Back lining (cut 2)

"Elegance is elimination."

Cristóbal Balenciaga

Figure 4.11
Close-up of skirt detail.

The Wrap Dress

Patterning concepts learned

- Wrap-around style line
- Neckline contouring
- Transferring darts to hemline
- Single to multiple dart conversion
- Circular ruffled collar with bias binding
- Armhole facing
- Combined curved front and hem facing
- Back hem facing

Figure 5.1
Designed wrap dress.

The History of the Wrap Dress

The jersey wrap dress is so closely identified with fashion designer Diane von Furstenberg that many people don't realize it was deeply embedded in American identity long before her interpretation of it. From Elsa Schiaparelli's and Charles James's versions in the 1930s to Claire McCardell's original "popover" dress in the 1940s, women have been wearing the wrap dress in one form or another for years.

Von Furstenberg is said to have designed her iconic wrap dress in 1974 in the spirit of enabling women to enjoy sexual freedom, and the dress does indeed have a perceived feminist significance. But interestingly, one of the best-known versions of the wrap dress is the Hooverette, a simple housedress from the 1930s, which exemplified the opposite association.

The Hooverette's popularity was due to its practicality. The wrap style allowed the front to be reversible, so when the front of the dress became dirty the wrap could be reversed to reveal the clean underside. The Hooverette's name is thought to be a derivation of the "Hoover apron"—an artifact from before the First World War when Herbert Hoover ran the Federal Food Administration. This wrapped-apron style transformed into a lady's day dress soon after. The efficient design of the dress included all the features of a conventional dress, but was intended to be worn only inside the house. The washable cotton print dress appealed to all shapes and sizes, and was not only utilitarian to wear but also stylishly appropriate in case someone happened to stop by for a visit.

The Swirl dress, a descendant of the Hooverette originally called Neat 'n' Tidy, was another version of the domestic wrap. It was created in the early 1940s by L. Nachman and Sons Company. The Swirl was sold as a quick and easy dress for the busy homemaker to slip into. Ethel on the television show *I Love Lucy* famously wore several different incarnations of the Swirl dress, and undoubtedly inspired many other 1950s' homemakers to do the same.

Domestic variations aside, the wrap also has a strong association with the American ready-to-wear industry. Charles James's 1932 version in wool rib knit was named

the "taxi" dress because a woman could easily put it on in the back of a taxi. (Now that's something to ponder!) James, known for his complex design ideas, created this seemingly simple dress with minimal seams. Made in only two sizes, it is credited as being the first dress to be sold alongside sweaters in the accessories department at the Best & Co. department store. The dress was considered one of James's most important designs, both critically and commercially, and helped to establish what was to become known as the "American Look" during the 1940s.

Figure 5.2
Vintage pattern for Hooverette dress, 1940s.

The 1940s was known as the "Golden Age" of American sportswear. In previous decades American designers were mostly unknown, and the practice was to copy the fashions of Paris. With the advent of the Second World War, the United States was cut off from European fashions and the time was ripe for American designers to shine. Claire McCardell, often credited with popularizing the "American Look," believed that clothing should be functional, stylish, and also easy to wear. In 1942 McCardell designed the "popover," a simple denim wrap-around dress that could be "popped over" just about anything and also worn alone. The dress was an instant success, and a variation of the design was incorporated into all her future collections, making it one of her most recognized styles.

The iconic wrap dress designed by von Furstenberg actually got its start as a two-piece. According to von Furstenberg, "It started as a wrap top and skirt, and I thought it would make a simple and sexy dress. I had no idea it would be such a phenomenon." The Belgian-born designer, who moved to New York in 1970, designed the long-sleeved knit jersey dress in 1974 as a reinterpretation of the classic kimono design. The dress was an instant hit, and came to symbolize the liberation and empowerment of a whole new generation of women. By 1976 more than 5 million dresses had been sold and the 29-year-old was featured on the cover of *Newsweek* magazine. Von Furstenberg reintroduced the iconic dress in 1997, and it has been a featured design in her collections ever since.

The appeal of the wrap lies in its minimal construction, and it is a dress that anyone can wear with confidence and timeless style.

Figure 5.3
Designer Claire McCardell in her studio wearing a popover dress of her own design, 1940.

Figure 5.4
Fashion designer Diane von Furstenberg with artist Andy Warhol and actor Monique Van Vooren at the New York City premiere of the film *Flesh for Frankenstein*, 1974.

"I didn't really know what I wanted to do, but I knew the woman I wanted to become."

Diane von Furstenberg

Contemporary Wrap Dresses

The traditional wrap has exceeded its original home-makers' symbolism and Studio 54 vibe to become a modern essential.

Figure 5.5
Yohji Yamamoto, Runway, Paris Fashion Week, Spring/Summer 2020.

Figure 5.6
Alexander McQueen, Runway, Paris Fashion Week, Fall/Winter 2018/2019.

The Pattern

Start with front torso contour and back torso blocks

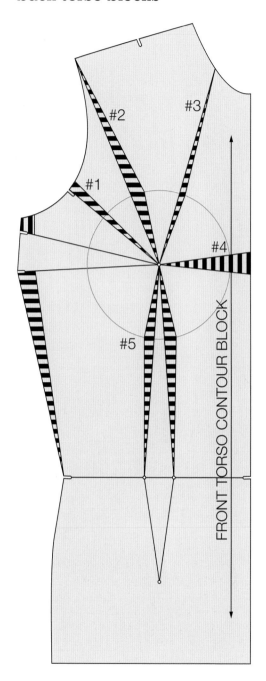

#2

#3

#1

#4

#5

FRONT TORSO CONTOUR BLOCK

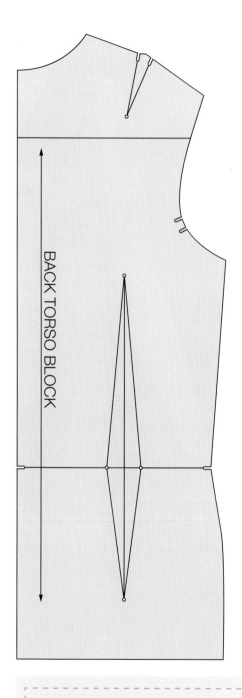

BACK TORSO BLOCK

AUTHOR TIP

Patterning directions for the front torso contour block are in the "Blocks Identified" section in the Introduction of this book.

Lengthen front pattern, front wrap extension, and neckline development

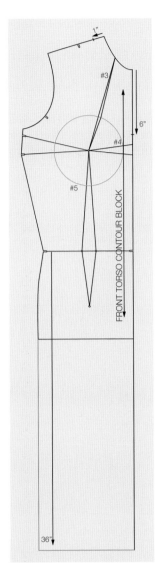

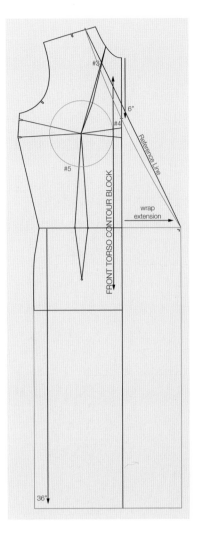

1. Trace front torso contour block, transferring markings for guidelines 3 and 4.

AUTHOR TIP

Note: Patterning directions for the front torso with side-bust dart block is in the **Blocks Identified** section of the book.

---

1. Lengthen pattern 36 inches (90 cm) from waist. **Note: You can extend the length as much or as little as you prefer.**
2. Open neckline up by 1 inch (2.5 cm).

3. Mark 6 inches (15 cm) down from neckline. **Note: This is the depth of the V-neck; you can adjust depth if you wish.**
4. Measure front waist and record_____. Don't forget to subtract the dart intake in the measurement!
5. For wrap extension, extend the center front (CF) by two-thirds of the front waistline measurement and square down to hem. **Note: You want to make sure there is enough excess fabric for the wrap, to ensure the dress stays closed when sitting.**
6. Draw new neckline, connecting new neckline to waist passing through the CF depth.
7. Place ruler on new neckline and draw a line to the waist. **Note: This is your reference line.**
8. Using a hip curve, draw a curved neckline passing through all points.

Contouring front neckline

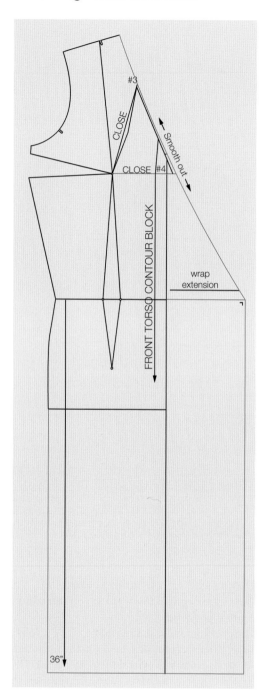

1. Transfer contour guidelines 3 and 4 to the side-bust dart using the slash-and-spread method.
2. Extend contouring guideline 4 to the edge of the neckline.
3. Cut guidelines 3 and 4 to the edge of the bust point (apex).
4. Cut side-bust dart leg to the edge of the bust point (apex).
5. Close guidelines 3 and 4 and tape shut. **Note: Close them as you would a dart. Don't worry if the dart legs don't fully match up on guideline 3.**
6. Smooth out neckline curve.

Transfer side-bust dart to shoulder and hem

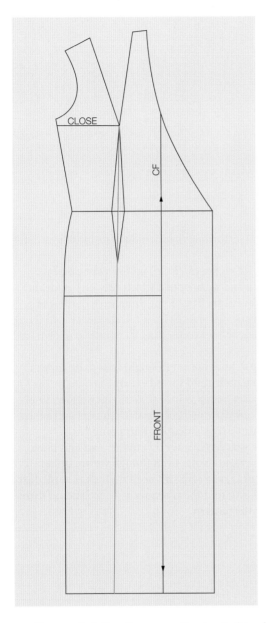

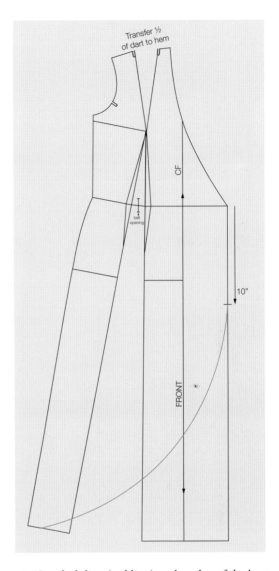

1. Draw a slash line from apex (bust point) to shoulder notch.
2. Cut slash line to the edge of the bust point (apex).
3. Cut side-bust dart leg to the edge of the bust point (apex).
4. Close side-bust dart and tape shut.
5. Measure shoulder dart width and record_____.
6. Draw a slash line (red line) through mid-point of contour dart.
7. Transfer half of shoulder dart to hem using the slash-and-spread method.
8. Cut slash line (red line) to the edge of the bust point (apex).
9. Transfer half of the shoulder dart width to the hemline and secure.
10. Mark 10 inches (25 cm) down from waist at front extension.
11. Curve front skirt to desired shape (red curved line).
12. Mark belt opening at the waist using the measurement you used for the wrap extension (two-thirds of the front waist measurement).
13. To mark the placement for the belt opening on the pattern, draw a vertical line equal to the belt width plus ⅛ inch (3 mm) for ease, as shown. The belt is 1½ inches (3.75 cm) wide. **Note: This will only be used on the right side of the dress.**

Dart-tuck grouping at shoulder

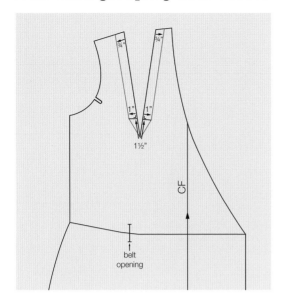

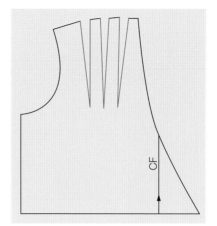

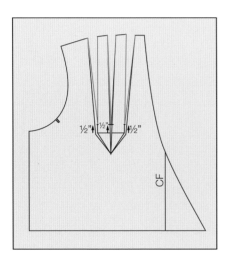

1. We will be turning the shoulder dart into three dart-tucks.
2. Mark 1½ inches (3.75 cm) up from apex on each dart leg and square out a 1 inch (2.5 cm) guideline.
3. Mark out ¾ inch (1.75 cm) from each dart leg at shoulder.
4. Draw slash lines connecting all points, as shown (red lines).
5. Cut slash lines to (not through) bust point (apex), secure pattern, and spread evenly.
6. Mark dart points ½ inch (1.2 cm) above slash lines, draw new darts using the inside dart leg, and adjust the outside leg to meet the dart point.
7. Divide space evenly for the middle dart and draw new dart legs. **Note: Even though we are doing dart-tucks, you will still need to draft the full darts in order to fold them properly when trueing them up on the pattern.**

Converting darts to dart-tucks

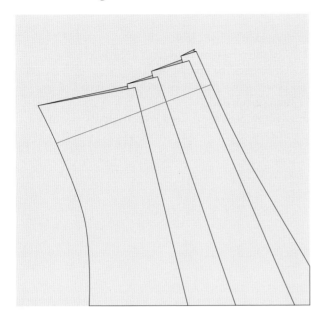

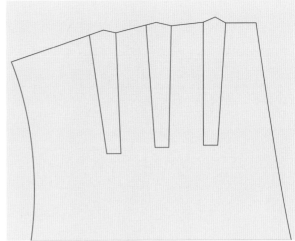

1. Fold darts toward CF to close.
2. Score the dart leg with an awl closest to the direction in which you are folding the dart.
3. Close the pattern by placing the dart point (not the bust point!) on the side corner of the table, match up the dart legs, and tape down.
4. While the pattern is still closed, mark the tuck closest to the CF 3 inches (7.5 cm) down on the dart closest to the neckline.
5. Place a ruler perpendicular to the dart leg at the mark and draw a line through all darts. This will be the end of the stitching line for the dart-tucks.
6. Cut the shoulder seam while the pattern is still folded.
7. Open pattern up and connect ends of dart-tucks, as shown.

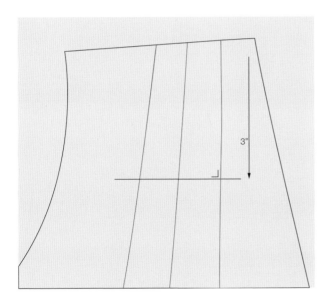

Lengthen back pattern and neckline development

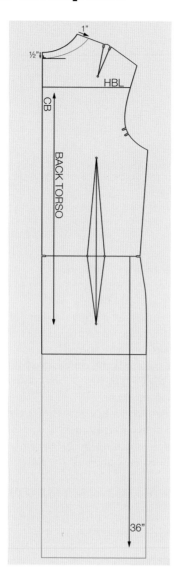

1. Trace back torso block.
2. Lengthen pattern 36 inches (90 cm) from waist.
3. Open neckline up by 1 inch.
4. Lower center back (CB) neckline ½ inch (1.2 cm) and square out.
5. Redraw neckline using a French curve (red curved line).

Transfer shoulder dart to hem

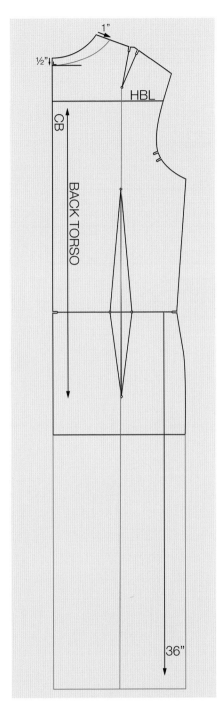

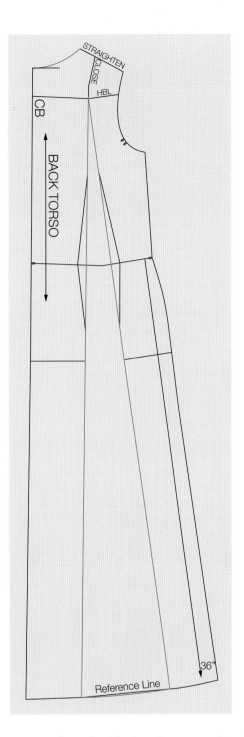

1. Square a slash line down from the shoulder dart point, passing through the mid-point of the contour dart to the hem.
2. Close shoulder dart using the slash-and-spread method, with the horizontal balance line (HBL) as the slash point.

3. Straighten shoulder line if necessary. Retain shoulder notch.
   Note: The sweep of the hem may need to be adjusted. Wait until the muslin (toile) fitting to determine if adjustments need to be made.

Wrap belts

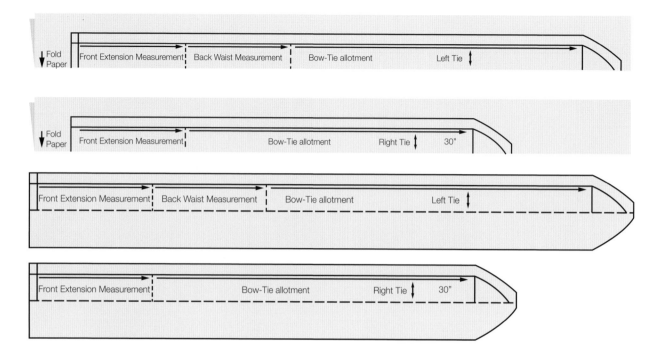

1. Fold two pieces of pattern paper in half.
2. Mark up 1½ inches (3.75 cm).
3. For the right-side belt, add front extension measurement plus 30 inches (75 cm) for bow.
4. For the left-side belt, add the back waist measurement plus front extension measurement plus 36 inches (90 cm) for bow. **Note: The left belt is 6 inches (15 cm) longer so the bow-tie will be even after the belt is tied.**
5. Finish the end of the bow by curving the edge as shown.
6. Add ½ inch (1.2 cm) seam allowance (SA) to the length of the belt.
7. Add ¼ inch (6 mm) SA to end of the belt.
8. Notch edge of belt and fold lines.

AUTHOR TIP

I have added SA here to simplify production pattern development.

Muslin or Toile Fitting

- Before you draft the lining patterns, prepare a muslin for fit.
- Do not add SA to pattern, as you will most likely be adjusting the muslin for fit.

- Draw the SA directly on to the muslin after tracing the working pattern.
- Make any necessary fit corrections to the pattern.
- Now you can move on to the lining patterns.

> **AUTHOR TIP**
>
> Note: You can either sew or pin muslin. I chose to sew this muslin to help ensure a proper fit on the form.
>
> Fit the dress before you make the neckline ruffles to ensure that enough ease has been taken out of the neckline. After you test fit the muslin (toile), attach the ruffles for a final fit.

Figure 5.8
Close-up of muslin ruffle.

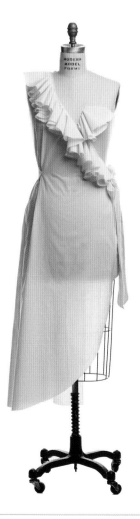

Figure 5.7
Checking muslin fit.

Circular neckline ruffled collar

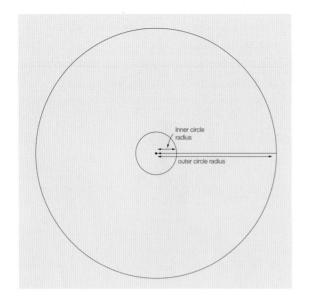

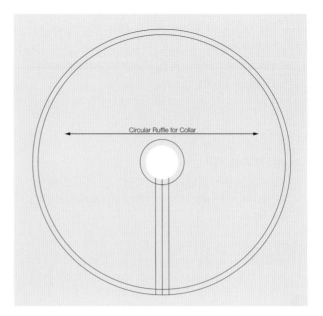

Circular Ruffle for Collar

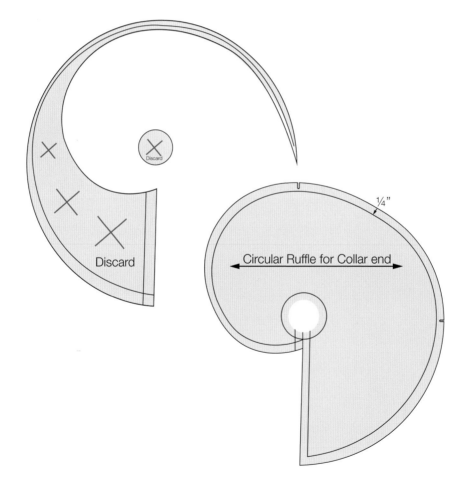

Inner circle radius

outer circle radius

Discard

Discard

Circular Ruffle for Collar end

¼"

1. We need to find the inner-circle circumference (stitching line) for the ruffles.
2. Measure front neckline and record_____.
3. Measure front V-neck depth of shoulder to CF plus 1 inch (2.5 cm), and record_____.
4. Measure back neckline and multiply by two; record_____.
   Note: You want the ruffle to stop at the V-neck depth for the left side, as it wraps under the right side of the dress bodice.
5. Add the front V-neck depth and back neckline measurements together, plus 3½ inches (8.76 cm) for the SAs: 19¾ inches (49.25 cm) + 9¾ inches (24.76 cm) + 8½ inches (21.59 cm) + 3½ inches (8.76 cm) = 41½ inches (105.41 cm). **Note: I am using the measurements for my neckline as an example.**
6. This measurement needs to be divided by the number of circles you are using: 41½ inches (105.41 cm) ÷ 7 = 5.92 inches (14.82 cm). This is the stitching line or circumference of the inner section of the circle (including the SA to connect the individual circles together—this is the part of the ruffle that will be stitched to the neckline).

Now for the math! We need to calculate the radius of the circle to make things easier. The radius of a circle is equal to its circumference divided by 2 pi.

Fortunately, you can find a circumference calculator online. I plugged in my circumference of 5.92 inches (14.82 cm) and my radius equals 0.942 inches, rounded up to 1 inch (2.5 cm), with the diameter 2 inches (5 cm). **Note: I rounded this to 1 inch (2.5 cm) because the difference is minimal.**

7. Make a circle using a compass tool.
8. Mark the radius measurement and draw the inner circle.
9. The width of the ruffle is 4 inches (10 cm)—or whatever you choose.
10. You will need to add the width of the ruffle to the radius to get the outer-circle radius measurement. This measurement is 5 inches (12.7 cm).
11. Make a copy of the ruffle and curve edges, as shown, as two of the circle's edges will curve for a more flattering effect where the collar ends.
12. Add ¼ inch (6 mm) SA to both the inner and outer circles, as well as to the cutting line where the circles will be sewn together. Tip: Use your compass for this too! Discard inner circles. **Note: I have added the SA here to simplify things**.

Armhole facing, combined curved front and hem facing, and back hem facing

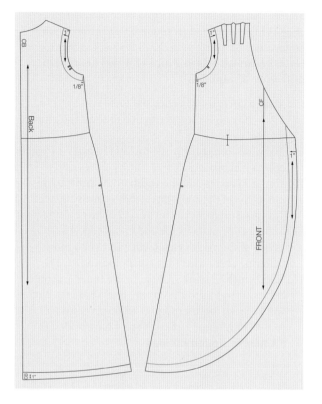

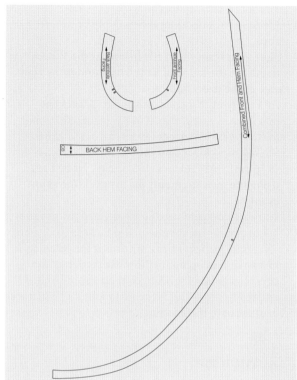

1. For facings, measure in 1 inch (2.5 cm) on front skirt, back hemline, and front and back armholes, as shown (red curved lines).
2. Bring side-seam of front and back armholes in ⅛ inch (3 mm), and blend to zero at notches.
   Note: You reduce the facing pieces to ensure they fit snugly to the body.
3. Draw grain lines parallel to CF and CB.

Neckline bias binding

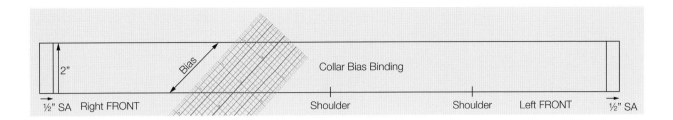

Production Pattern
Seam Allowances and Hems

AUTHOR TIP

Before adding SAs and hems, be sure to walk your patterns and make any necessary corrections if seams and/or control notches do not match up.

Front and back pattern seam allowance and hems

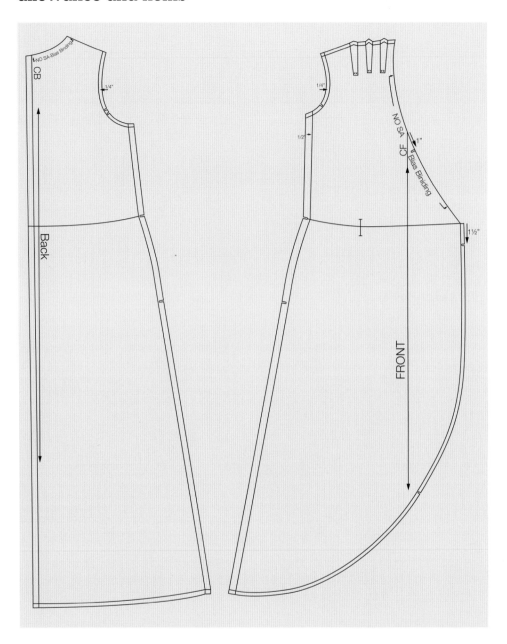

1. Add ½ inch (1.2 cm) SA to back seam, shoulder and side-seams. **Note: You can omit the CB seam if your fabric is wide enough.**
2. Add ¼ inch (6 mm) to front and back armholes, front skirt, and back hem.
3. Do not add SA to the front and back necklines, as they are bias bound.
4. Notch 1 inch (2.5 cm) down from CF for ruffle placement for the left side.
5. Circle and drill (red circles) ⅛ inch (3 mm) in and up on dart-tucks.

Armhole facing, combined curved front and hem facing, and back hem facing seam allowances

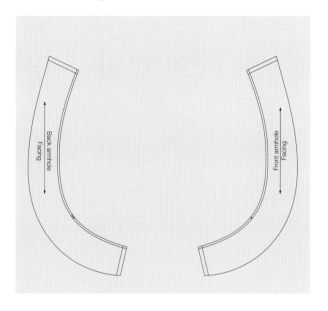

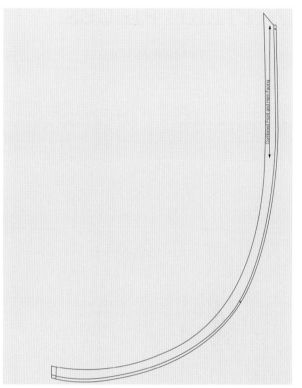

1. For back hem, fold pattern paper and trace back hem facing.
2. Add ½ inch (1.2 cm) SA to shoulder seams and side-seams.
3. Add ¼ inch (6 mm) SA to front skirt and back hemline.
4. You do not add SA to the armhole facings, as they are bias bound.

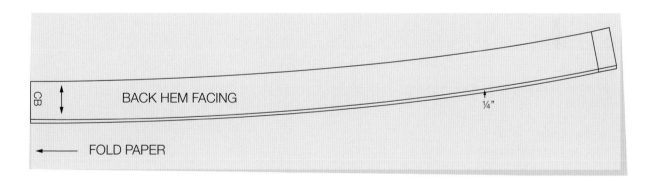

TECHNICAL FLATS AND FINISHED PATTERN PIECES

Technical flat front

Technical flat back

Self

1. Front (cut 1).
2. Side-front (cut 2).
3. Back (cut 2).
4. Side-back (cut 2).
5. Bandeau collar (cut 2).
6. Armhole bias binding (cut 2).

"It's not about the dress you wear, but it's about the life you lead in the dress."

Diana Vreeland

Figure 5.9
Ruffle detail.

The Strapless Dress

Patterning concepts learned

- Strapless contouring principles
- Princess style line bodice with attached A-line skirt
- Corselette foundation with waist stay
- Combined bodice facing
- Lining patterns

Figure 6.1
Designed strapless dress front.

Figure 6.1A
Strapless back dress/corselette
detail.

The History of the Strapless Dress

The strapless dress, a mainstay in today's fashion industry, at first glance seems to defy gravity, as there are no visible means of support. A glance inside at the dress's construction helps to demystify the style: it is the internal corset built into the dress that helps to keep it in place. Known more today as the go-to look for brides and black-tie events, the strapless has an intriguing position in fashion's history with its storied past.

Mainbocher, the American couturier in Paris, is believed to have introduced the first strapless evening dress to the public in 1934. It is said that Mainbocher's dress, cut in black satin, was inspired by John Singer Sargent's 1884 portrait of Madame X (Madame Pierre Gautreau). When shown at the Paris Salon the same year, the portrait was more ridiculed than admired—so much so that Sargent kept the painting in his own private collection for over 30 years. He eventually sold it to the Metropolitan Museum of Art in New York in 1916, commenting, "I suppose it is the best thing I have done."

It should be noted that four years before Mainbocher's debut of the strapless dress, American singer and actress Libby Holman was photographed wearing the style and is frequently credited with inventing it. Holman, known more for her exploits off the stage than her performances on it, was accused of killing her first husband, tobacco heir Z. Smith Reynolds, in 1932. Her notorious personal life created such a frenzy in the news that in 1935 a film, *Reckless*, starring Jean Harlow, was based on her scandalous life.

American socialite and heiress Brenda Frazier's 1938 cover photo on *Life* magazine, in which she is wearing a strapless gown, is said to have helped popularize the style. Frazier was known as one of the Great Depression's "glamour girls." She and her contemporaries, deemed the "poor little rich girls," appeared regularly in the gossip columns of the day with reports of their charmed and glamorous lives. The masses, eager for some happy news, were drawn to their fairytale existence. Frazier's debutante ball was so highly publicized worldwide that, remarkably, this was the sole reason why she appeared on *Life*'s cover.

Socialites aside, it was Rita Hayworth's performance in the 1946 film *Gilda* that cemented the look for generations to come. Her black satin gown, designed by Jean Louis, became known as the "Put the Blame on Mame" dress, referring to the song that was playing during an infamous and racy scene.depicting Hayworth's character singing and dancing with overt sexual overtones. The fact that the dress stayed in place while Gilda fervently moved about the stage is not only a tribute to its internal structure and construction, but also proved once and for all that the strapless dress was indeed wearable.

Often referred to as the "naked" look, Catholic campaigners in the United States actually protested against the style in the 1940s and 1950s, saying that it was immodest. A glimpse at any of the elegant strapless creations created by designers such as Charles James and Madame Grès during that time proves this to be untrue.

A more casual knit version of the strapless dress was introduced by Halston in the 1970s. The fabric kept the dress in place, thus eliminating the need for an inner structure. With no need for the corset, the style became a popular form of ready-to-wear, as it was

Figure 6.2
Madame X (Madame Pierre Gautreau) painting by John Singer Sargent, 1884.

easy to produce and hinted at the sexual liberation of the women who sported the look.

Due to its complexities of design, the original strapless dress is now mostly worn for special occasions and shows up consistently on the red carpet. Since the 1980s the dress has become a mainstay in the bridal industry, with a majority of brides choosing the style. Whether intentional or not, here's hoping that an individual in a strapless dress is in someway channeling the spirit of Gilda's sexy inner vamp!

Figure 6.4
Debutante Brenda Frazier in a strapless gown, 1938.

Figure 6.3
Actress Libby Holman in a strapless gown, 1930.

Figure 6.5
Actress Rita Hayworth performing in a scene from the film *Gilda*, 1946.

"I have never known a really chic woman whose appearance was not, in large part, an outward reflection of her inner self."

Mainbocher

Contemporary Strapless Dresses

Modern versions show that the strapless can be much more than a wedding dress.

Figure 6.6
Rochas, Runway, Paris Fashion Week, Spring/ Summer 2020.

Figure 6.7
Dries Van Noten, Runway, Paris Fashion Week, Spring/Summer 2020.

The Pattern

Start with front and back torso contour, front and back bodice contour, and front and back skirt blocks

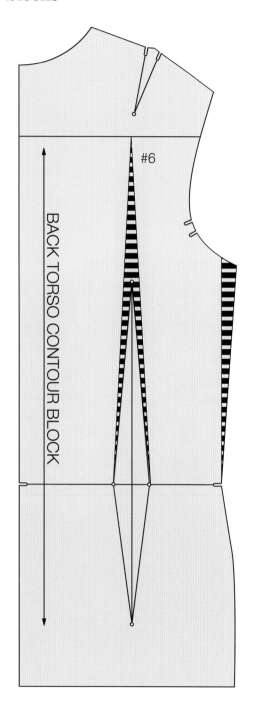

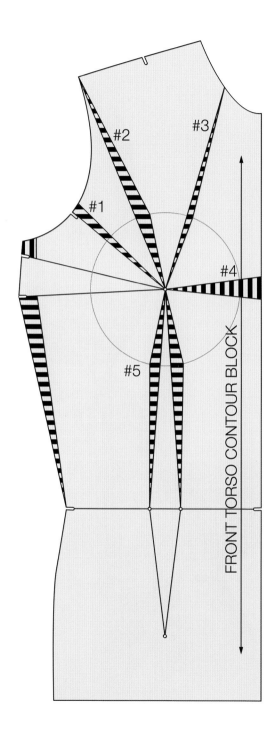

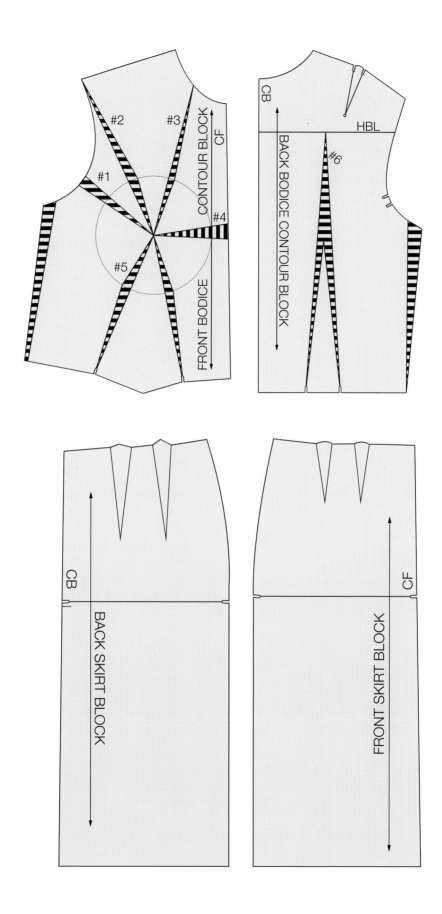

Add bodice contour blocks and skirt blocks

Corselette foundation

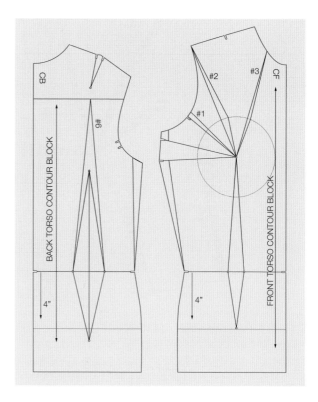

1. Trace contour pattern on front and back blocks.
2. Transfer guidelines 1, 2, and 3 and side-seam intake on front pattern.
3. Transfer guideline 6 and side-seam guideline on back pattern.
4. Shorten torso so it ends 4 inches (10 cm) below the waist on both front and back patterns.

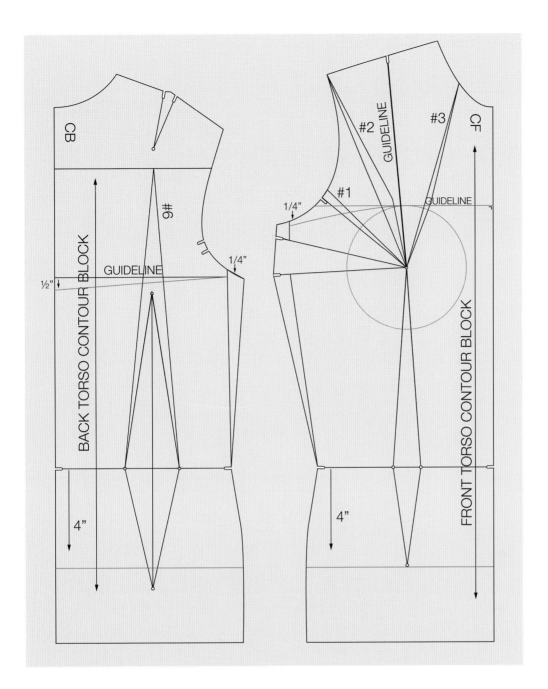

1. On front pattern, square a guideline from center front (CF), passing through top bust circumference.
2. Draw a curved line (red curved line) starting at the CF guideline, touching the top of the bust circumference, and ending ¼ inch (6 mm) below side-seam intake.
3. Draw a guideline from shoulder notch to bust point (apex) for princess style line development.
4. On the back pattern, mark ¼ inch (6 mm) below side-seam intake and square a guideline from center back (CB).
5. Mark ½ inch (1.2 cm) down from the guideline at CB.
6. Draw a curved line (red curved line) to connect the back to the side-seam.
7. Cut patterns from paper.

Front corselette princess style line development

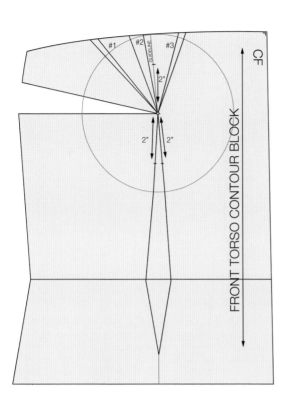

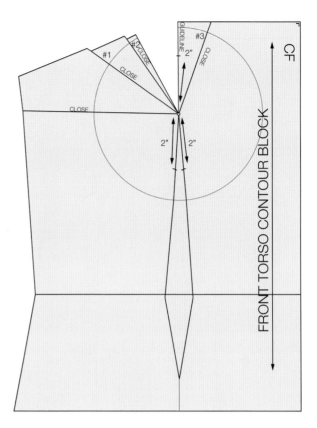

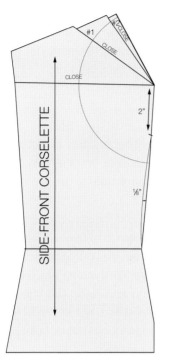

1. Extend a line (red line) from contour dart point to hemline.
2. Transfer contour guidelines and side-bust dart to princess guideline using the slash-and-spread method. **Note: You will be closing three guidelines and the side-bust dart, and transferring them into the princess guideline.**
3. Cut princess guideline to the edge of the bust point (apex).
4. Cut side-bust dart leg and contour guidelines 1, 2, and 3 to the edge of the bust point (apex).
5. Close side-bust and all contour guidelines and tape shut.
6. Mark control notches 2 inches (5 cm) above and below bust point (apex).
7. Cut front and side-front pieces apart making sure to cut out the contour dart.

8. Mark grainline on side-front perpendicular to waist.
9. Draw a ⅛ inch (3 mm) curve down both dart legs, starting at notches and ending at the waist, and cut out. **Note: This will adjust the contour under the bust for a snugger fit.**
10. Smooth out the bust line if it looks too pointy or uneven.
11. Walk the pattern from the waist up and waist down using an awl, adjusting the pattern as needed to balance style line at bodice top and hemline.
12. Straighten side-seam if necessary.
13. Mark 1 inch (2.5 cm) down CF and draw a curved sweetheart neckline, as shown.
14. Smooth out top neckline curve (red curve).

Back corselette princess style line development

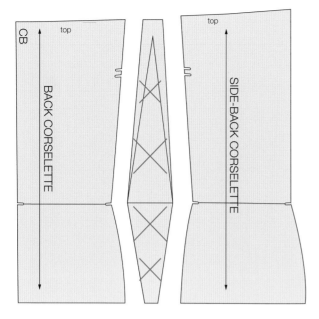

1. Cut back and side-back pieces apart using contour guideline 6, making sure to cut out the dart.
2. Mark grain line for side-back pattern perpendicular to waistline.
3. Notch waistline and a double notch for back.
4. Walk the pattern from the waist up and the waist down using an awl, adjusting the pattern as needed to balance the style line at bodice top and hemline.

Corselette Muslin or Toile Fitting

- Before you draft the dress pattern, prepare a full muslin for fitting the corselette.
- Do not add seam allowance (SA) to pattern, as you will most likely be adjusting the muslin for fit.
- Draw the SA directly on to the muslin after tracing the working pattern.
- Attach a zipper at CB to aid in fitting.
- The back zipper closure for the corselette will extend 5 inches (12.5 cm) beyond the garment so the wearer can get the corselette over the hips.
- Make any necessary fit corrections to the corselette pattern.
- A small contour dart is usually needed between the bust points (apex) at the CF so the corselette can hug the body. Pinch out the desired amount of fabric and sew the contour dart, ending 1 inch (2.5 cm) from the bust point (apex). **Note: This type of dart is called a Hollywood dart; not shown here.**
- Construct the corselette in the final fabric before moving on to the dress patterns.

Figure 6.8B
Back corselette muslin fit.

Figure 6.8A
Front corselette muslin fit.

Corselette Production Patterns

Front, side-front, back, and side-back corselette seam
allowances and boning placement

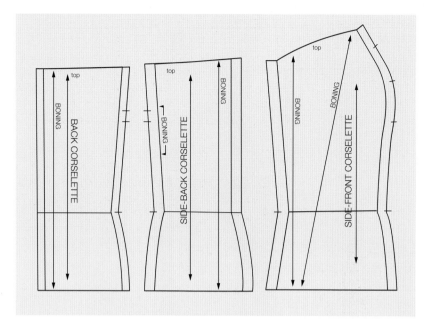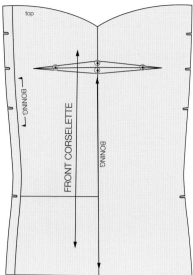

1. Fold pattern paper in half for the front pattern piece.
2. Add ½ inch (1.2 cm) SA to all seams with the exception of the top and bottom bodice.
3. Do not add SAs to top and bottom, as they will be bias bound.

Boning placement

The placement of the boning can vary depending on the shape of the model and the fit you want to achieve. Start with these guidelines, and add more boning if needed to get the desired shape. If the corselette fits snugly but is still not completely smooth in certain areas, add more boning.

- Place boning at the CF, stopping at the Hollywood (contour) dart.
- Place boning over the side-front and side-back seams.
- Place boning on either side of the side-seams.
- Place boning approximately ½ inch (1.2 cm) from the CB.
- Angle boning on side-front, as shown; this helps to create cleavage.

Researching proper ways of constructing a strapless dress, I have found that there are many different methods. Depending on the weight of the shell fabric and how it needs to be supported, you have a choice of fabrics to use for the corselette. In many couture garments, cotton bobbinet, a plain-weave silk, or cotton coutil (which is used when building a corset) can be used for the inner structure with spiral steel bones. Power net, a nylon/spandex blend, can also be used. It is essential that the corselette fabric is strong enough to do its intended job, which is to keep the shape of the dress and defy gravity. **Note: Rigilene boning can be used, but as it only bends in one direction it won't conform to the shape of the body as well as steel bones.**

The corselette closure here is a zipper which extends 5 inches (12.5 cm) beyond it. Another option is to use hooks and eyes instead of a zipper. If you choose to do this, make sure to sew in a placket to keep the hooks and eyes from digging into the skin.

The Dress Pattern
Front and back dress bodice

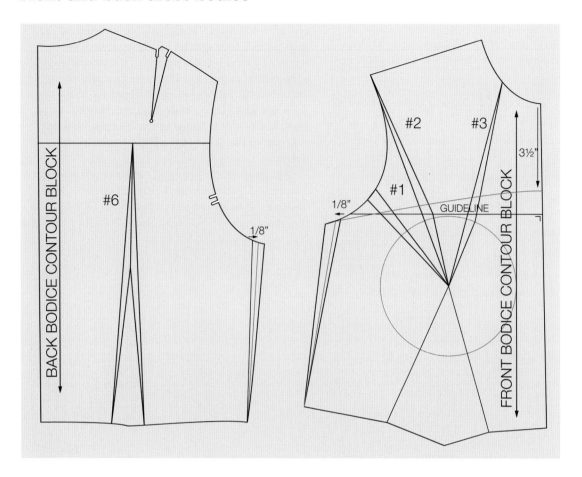

1. Trace front bodice and back bodice contour blocks. **Note: The torso block was used for the corselette even though the dress has a waistline seam. Extending the length of the foundation piece will ensure a solid base for the dress and also help to shape the silhouette.**
2. Reduce side-seam intake by ⅛ inch (3 mm).

3. Square a guideline from CF passing through top bust circumference.
4. Mark 3½ inches (8.75 cm) down from CF.
5. Draw a curved line for top bodice style line, as shown, starting at the side-seam intake, making sure to draw it above the CF guideline. **Note: The corselette at the bodice top is lower than the dress bodice to ensure it is concealed when wearing.**

> **AUTHOR TIP**
>
> As the dress sits directly on top of the corselette, the bodice needs to be a bit larger to allow for the boning, etc. Always fit the dress over the corselette, and adjust fit as needed by adding to or reducing the style lines.

Front bodice princess style line development

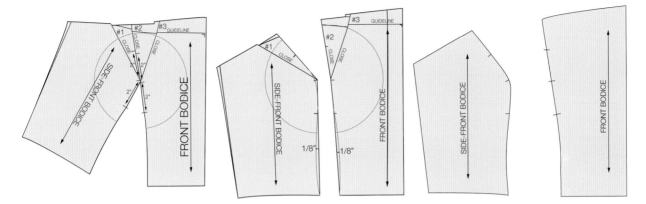

1. Transfer waist dart from contour guidelines using the slash-and-spread method.
2. Cut the princess guideline to the edge of the bust point (apex).
3. Cut contour guidelines 1, 2, and 3 to the edge of the bust point (apex).
4. Close all contour guidelines and tape shut.
5. Mark control notches 2 inches (5 cm) above and below the bust point (apex).
6. Cut through guideline 2 to separate the front and side-front bodice.
7. Mark grain line on side-front perpendicular to waist, as shown.
8. Draw a ⅛ inch (3 mm) curve down both dart legs, starting at notches and ending at the waist, and cut out. **Note: This will adjust the contour under the bust for a snugger fit.**
9. Smooth out the bust line if it looks too pointy or uneven.
10. Walk the pattern from the waist up and the waist down using an awl, adjusting the pattern as needed to balance the style line at bodice top and hemline.
11. Smooth out top bodice curve, as shown.

Back bodice princess style line development

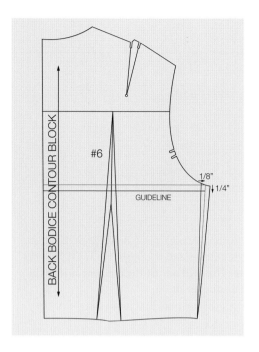

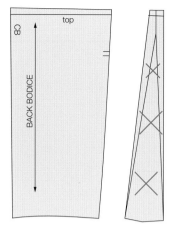

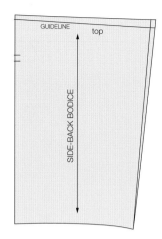

1. On back pattern, mark ¼ inch (6 mm) below side-seam intake and square a guideline from CB.
2. Mark ½ inch (1.2 cm) down from guideline at CB.
3. Draw style line (red curved line) above the guideline to connect back to side-seam.
4. Cut back and side-back pieces apart using contour guideline 6, making sure to cut out the dart.
5. Mark grain line for the side-back pattern perpendicular to waistline.
6. Notch waistline and mark a double notch for the back.
7. Walk the pattern from the waist up and the waist down using an awl, adjusting the pattern as needed to balance the style line at bodice top and hemline.

A-line skirt

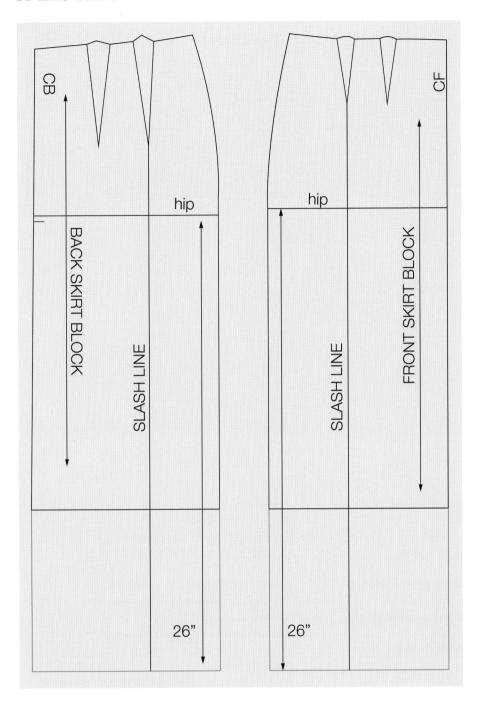

1. Trace the front and back skirt blocks.
2. Lengthen skirt 26 inches (65 cm) from hip to both front and back patterns. **Note: You can extend the length as much or as little as you prefer.**
3. Square a slash line from the hem to the dart point closest to the side-seam.

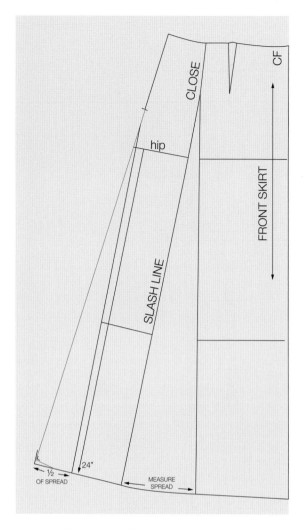

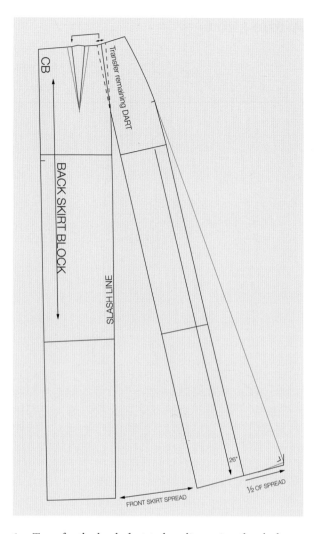

1. Transfer the front dart to hemline using the slash-and-spread method.
2. Cut slash line to the edge of the dart point.
3. Cut dart leg to the edge of the dart point.
4. Close dart and tape shut.
5. Measure the spread of the transferred front dart at the hemline and record_____.
6. Add half of the spread measurement to the front side-seam.
7. Square off the side-seam so it has the same hip-to-hem measurement.

1. Transfer the back dart to hemline using the slash-and-spread method.
2. Cut slash line to the edge of the dart point.
3. Cut dart leg to the edge of the dart point.
4. Close dart until the hemline spread for the back equals the front spread, and tape shut.
5. Transfer the excess dart to the remaining dart if needed.
6. You will have to shift the back dart over so that it will still match the princess line seam for the bodice. **Note: Depending on the body type, the back dart spread can be less than the front dart spread; if this is the case, you will need to transfer a portion of the remaining back dart to the hemline so the hemline spreads are equal.**

AUTHOR TIP

For the skirt to be balanced, you want the front and back hemline sweep to be equal. Occasionally, when transferring the front and back darts to the hemline, the spreads are equal and no adjustment needs to be made.

Muslin or Toile Fitting

- Before you draft the dress patterns, prepare a full muslin for fitting the dress.
- Do not add SA to pattern, as you will most likely be adjusting the muslin for fit.
- Draw the SA directly on to the muslin after tracing the working pattern.
- Add 1 inch (2.5 cm) SA to the bodice top for fitting purposes; this will allow for necessary adjustments to ensure the corselette doesn't show.
- Make any necessary fit corrections to the pattern with the finished corselette underneath—the dress should lie smoothly over the corselette.
- Now you can move on to the production patterns.

Figure 6.9
Checking muslin fit.

Front and back bodice facings and front, side-front, back, and side-back bodice linings

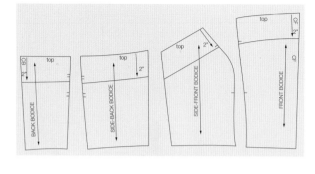

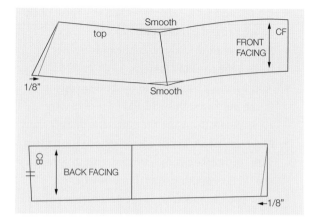

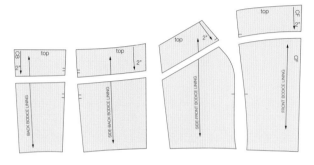

1. Trace front, side-front, back, and side-back pattern pieces.
2. Trace the top 2 inches (5 cm) of patterns for facing development and cut out, as shown.
3. Retain the bottom portions for the bodice lining patterns.

1. For facing pieces, place front, side-front, back, and side-back bodice pattern pieces together so they line up at the top and trace.
2. Smooth out as needed.
3. Reduce side-seam by ⅛ inch (3 mm) as shown, blending to original armhole seam.
4. Grain lines are parallel to CF and CB.

Front and back skirt lining

1. Trace front and back skirt pattern pieces for lining.

Production Pattern

Seam allowances and hems
Front, side-front, back, and side-back bodice seam allowance

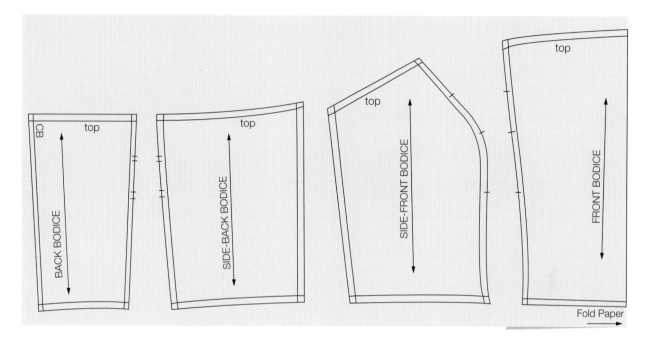

1. Fold paper in half and trace the front bodice pattern piece.
2. Trace the remaining bodice pattern pieces.
3. Add ½ inch (1.2 cm) SA to all seams with the exception of the top bodice neckline.
4. Add ¼ inch (6 mm) SA to the top bodice neckline.

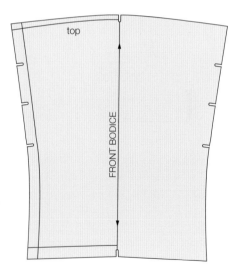

AUTHOR TIP

Before adding SAs and hems, be sure to walk your pattern and make any necessary corrections if seams or control notches do not match. Make sure that the skirt darts line up with the princess style lines on the waistline.

Front and back facing seam allowance

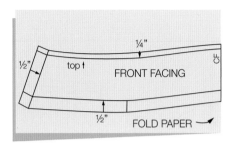

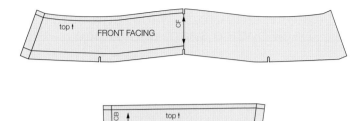

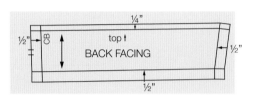

1. Fold paper in half and trace the front facing pattern piece.
2. Add ½ inch (1.2 cm) to all SAs with the exception of the top facing neckline.
3. Add ¼ inch (6 mm) SA to the top facing neckline.

Front, side-front, back, and side-back bodice lining seam allowances

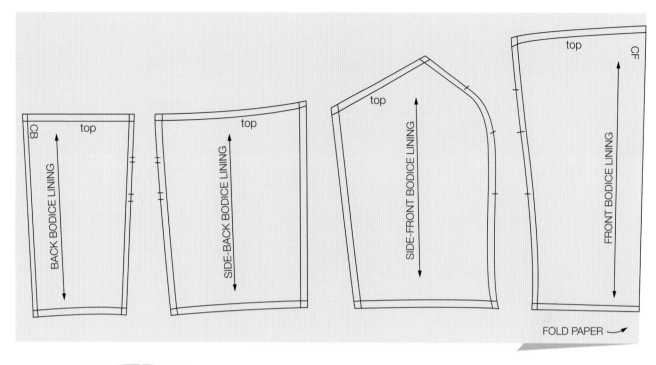

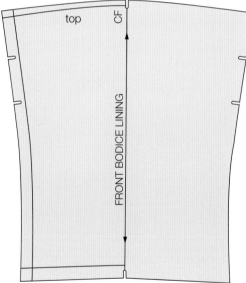

1. Fold paper in half and trace the front bodice lining pattern piece.
2. Trace the remaining bodice lining pattern pieces.
3. Add ½ inch (1.2 cm) SA to all seams.

Front and back skirt seam allowance and hems

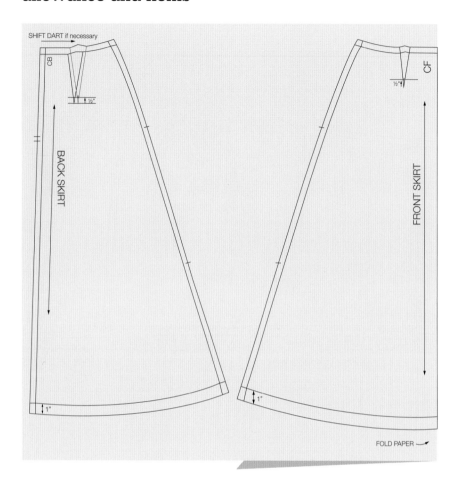

1. Fold paper in half and trace the front skirt pattern piece.
2. Trace the back skirt pattern piece.
3. Add ½ inch (1.2 cm) SA to all seams with the exception of the hem.
4. Mark hem 1 inch (2.5 cm).
5. If your pattern required moving one of the darts, make sure to shift the dart so it will align with the princess seams.
6. Circle and drill dart points ½ inch (1.2 cm) into the dart.

Front and back skirt lining seam allowance and hems

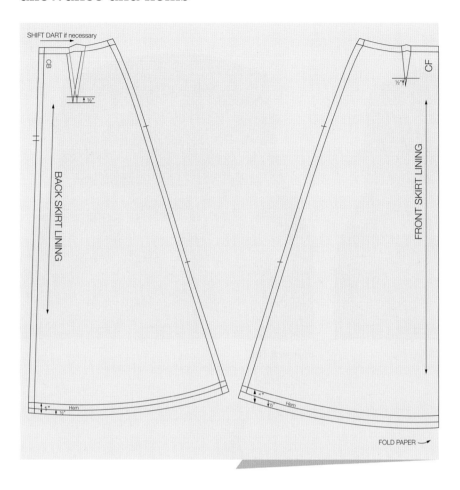

1. Fold paper in half and trace the front lining pattern piece.
2. Trace the back lining pattern piece.
3. Add ½ inch (1.2 cm) SA to all seams with the exception of the hem.
4. Lengthen skirt by ½ inch (1.2 cm).
5. Mark hem up 1 inch (2.5 cm) from new length.
6. If your pattern required moving one of the darts, make sure to shift the dart so it will align with the princess seams.
7. Circle and drill dart points ½ inch (1.2 cm) into the dart.

Constructing the Strapless Dress

Figure 6.10A
Dress back/corselette detail.

Figure 6.10B
Interior dress corselette construction detail with Hollywood dart.

Figure 6.10C
Dress back/corselette detail.

Figure 6.10D
Dress waist-stay detail.

The dress is layered from the inside out in this order.

1. Corselette.
2. Lining.
3. Dress shell.

Remember that the corselette is always a bit smaller than the dress it is supporting, and cannot be sewn in between the shell and lining to make the dress fit properly. It is generally attached to the outer dress at the waist with swing tacks, also known as French tacks, to keep the dress from shifting when wearing. It is hand-stitched to the facing at the bodice front and side-seams as needed.

Sometimes you will see the facing catch stitched on top of the corselette on the front of the dress—it seems that every designer has their own method, depending on the design. There are couture sewing books listed in the Bibliography that you can use as a reference for more sewing details. Claire Shaeffer's *Couture Sewing Techniques* (see Further Reading list) can be a great help.

Finally, a waist-stay is needed. A waist-stay is attached to the corselette and helps alleviate the strain on the closures. It also helps to keep the dress from shifting up when you are sitting down, hence the name. Petersham ribbon is used for the waist-stay. Not to be confused with grosgrain ribbon, Petersham ribbon will shape to the contours of the waist, whereas grosgrain ribbon will not. To make the waist-stay, measure the waist of the dress and cut the ribbon 4 inches (10 cm) longer than the waist measurement. Fold the ends of the ribbon back 1 inch (1.2 cm) and press. Fold the ribbon another inch (1.2 cm) and sew in place. Sew the ribbon to the inside of the corselette stopping 3–4 inches (7.5–10 cm) away from the CB. Make sure that the bottom of the ribbon is placed at the waistline, with the excess moving up toward the bust. If using steel boning, do not sew through the boning as it will break the needle! The last step is to sew two hooks and eyes on to the waist-stay.

TECHNICAL FLATS AND FINISHED PATTERN PIECES

Technical flat front

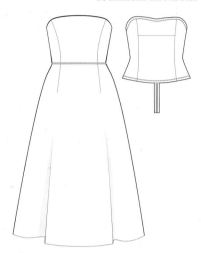

Technical flat back

Self
Front bodice (cut 1).
Side-front bodice (cut 2).
Back bodice (cut 2).
Side-back bodice (cut 2).
Front skirt (cut 1).
Back skirt (cut 2).
Front bodice facing (cut 1).
Back bodice facing (cut 2).

Interfacing
Front facing (cut 1).
Back facing (cut 2).

Corselette fabric
Front (cut 1).
Side-front (cut 2).
Back (cut 2).
Side-back (cut 2).

Lining
Front bodice (cut 1).
Side-front bodice (cut 2).
Back bodice (cut 2).
Side-back bodice (cut 2).
Front skirt (cut 1).
Back skirt (cut 2).

"People will stare. Make it worth their while."
Harry Winston

Figure 6.11
Dress interior construction detail.

The Shirtwaist Dress

Patterning concepts learned

- Bodice yoke
- Transferring darts to gathers
- Front facing with button extension
- Sleeve with extended gathered cap
- Convertible collar
- Front hip pocket
- Flared skirt
- Lining patterns

Figure 7.1
Designed shirtwaist dress.

The History of the Shirtwaist

The shirtwaist dress, which combines the elements of both a blouse and a skirt, was at its peak of popularity during the 1950s, but it was Christian Dior's "New Look" collection in 1947 that brought the style to the forefront of fashion. Also known as the "shirtmaker," its origin lies in the shirtwaist blouse and the American ready-to-wear industry. The shirtwaist embodied a new-found freedom and independence for the working women of the early twentieth century. A symbol of the suffragette movement, the blouse had been gaining in popularity since the mid-1850s and became an iconic image for the women's rights campaign. The original was modeled after men's dress shirts, and came to represent the feminist ideals of the working women of the time. These women, known as Gibson Girls in the United States, began wearing the simple cotton shirtwaist blouse as an alternative to the restrictive fashions of the previous era. This "New Woman," depicted in Charles Gibson's iconic drawings of the time, embodied the virtues of the liberated working woman, whose dress exemplified the personification of her ideals by combining fashion and reformation.

Tragically, it is a fire at the Triangle Waist Company in New York City in 1911 with which the shirtwaist is most closely associated and for which it is remembered. The epitome of a sweatshop, the factory's poor working conditions and the disrepair of its buildings contributed to 146 deaths when the mostly immigrant women workers became trapped and were unable to exit the factory due to broken elevators and locked doors. The fire drew widespread attention to the unsafe conditions in factories, and forever changed factory working conditions in the United States.

It was not until the 1930s that the shirtwaist actually became a dress. This iteration appeared as a sports dress for golf, tennis, and spectator sports. In 1935 the McMullen Company of Glens Falls, New York introduced a new line of "shirt-frocks" for women, tailored to look like men's dress shirts. In its adverts the following year the company dubbed the dress a "shirtmaker to women," which ultimately became known as the shirtwaist dress.

During the Second World War a narrow version of the shirtwaist dress became popular and was worn for most daily activities. Based on the "utility" look, its design conformed to the fabric restrictions for clothing implemented as part of the war effort.

The 1950s'-style shirtwaist was popularized by Christian Dior's "New Look" silhouette, introduced in 1947. The "New Look" focused on a small cinched waist with a full skirt, and was considered a breath of fresh air after the wartime fabric restrictions. To achieve Dior's ideal version of the dress, a woman needed specific undergarments: full petticoats and waist "waspies" helped to achieve the shirtwaist's silhouette. While Dior is the most noted designer to bring the shirtwaist to the forefront of fashion with his "Cherie" dress, it was American designer Claire McCardell's youthful version that made the style the go-to dress for women in the United States. Made in men's shirting fabrics, the dress was cut for comfort and was an ideal choice for the active woman on the go.

The dress was so popular in the 1950s that it became synonymous with the "middle-class" domestic lifestyle in the United States. Popular television shows at the time, such as *Leave It to Beaver* and *The Adventures of Ozzie and Harriet*, characterized a portrait of an American housewife who seemed to live in a version of the shirtwaist dress. These glorified depictions of the homemaker in her "uniform" helped to solidify an unattainable idealized version of women which reinforced the notion of "women's work." But by the mid-1960s the shirtwaist dress had taken a back seat in favor of a boxier shape in fashion.

Figure 7.2
Advertisement for shirtwaist sewing patterns, 1906.

In 1972, at the height of the women's liberation movement, designer Roy Halston reinvented the style. His version eliminated the waistline seam and was cut to resemble and elongate a man's shirt in a remarkable synthetic fabric known as Ultrasuede. Halston was known for his minimalistic approach to fashion, and the dress was sexy, comfortable, and helped to define a new casual American way of dressing. With Halston's reinterpretation of the dress, the shirtwaist came full circle back to its feminist roots and has remained a fashion staple to this day. The Gibson Girls of yesteryear would be proud.

Figure 7.4
Model in shirtwaist dress by Claire McCardell, 1946.

Figure 7.3
Woman wearing a utility shirtwaist dress in Britain during the Second World War, 1943.

Figure 7.5
Leave It to Beaver television program, 1957.

"You're only as good as the people you dress."

Halston

Contemporary Shirtwaists

An essential dress manifests itself as a must-have for every style tribe.

Figure 7.6
Celine, Runway, Paris Fashion Week, Fall/Winter 2019/2020.

Figure 7.6A
Rochas, Runway, Paris Fashion Week, Fall/Winter 2019/2020.

The Pattern

Start with basic bodice, sleeve, and skirt blocks

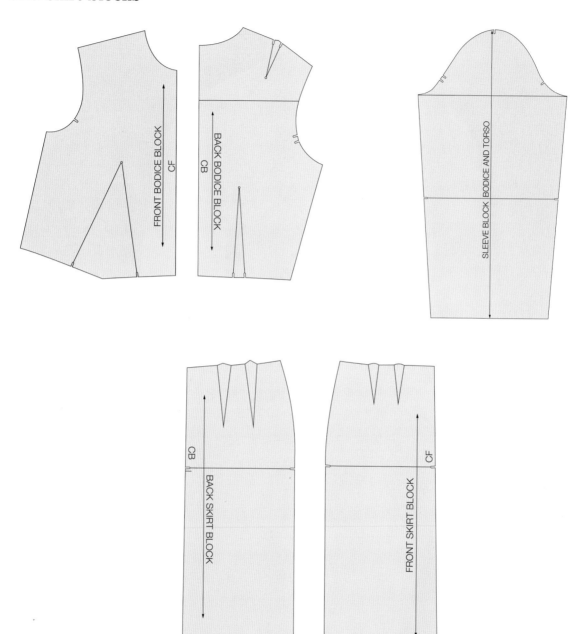

FRONT BODICE BLOCK

CF

BACK BODICE BLOCK

CB

SLEEVE BLOCK (BODICE AND TORSO)

CB

BACK SKIRT BLOCK

CF

FRONT SKIRT BLOCK

Bodice yoke

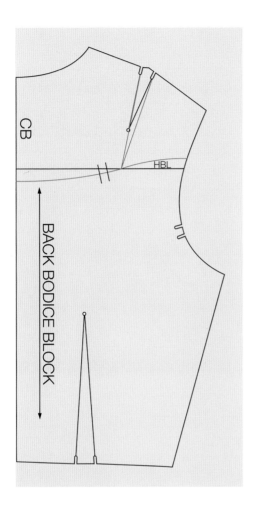

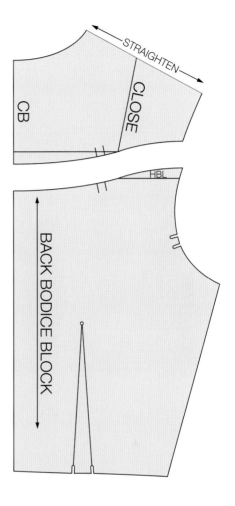

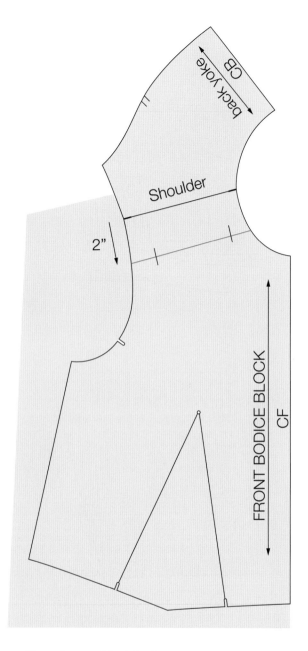

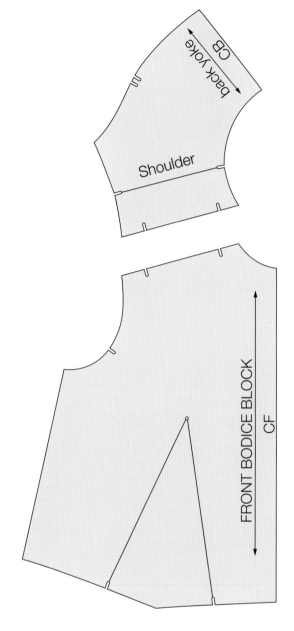

1. Trace front and back bodice patterns.
2. Measure front neckline and record_____.
3. Measure back neckline and record_____.
4. Extend back neck dart to the horizontal balance line (HBL).
5. For yoke, draw the desired curved line, making sure to pass through the back dart point (red curved line).
6. Notch yoke and cut pattern out.
7. Close neck dart using the slash-and-spread method.
8. Cut shoulder dart leg to the new dart point at the HBL.
9. Close shoulder dart and tape shut.
10. Smooth yoke curve and straighten shoulder if necessary.
11. Mark 2 inches (5 cm) down from shoulder on the front bodice and draw a line.
12. Place back portion of yoke and front bodice pattern pieces together at shoulder and secure.
13. Notch front yoke 1 inch (2.5 cm) in from neckline and armhole.
14. Notch shoulder seams, as shown.
15. Cut out the yoke.

Transferring front bodice dart into gathers and front extension

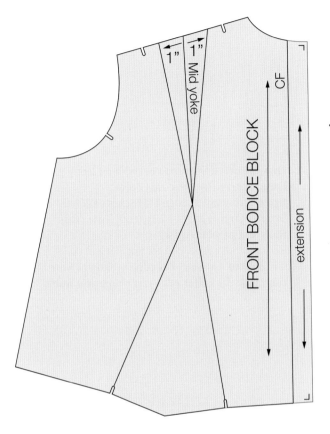

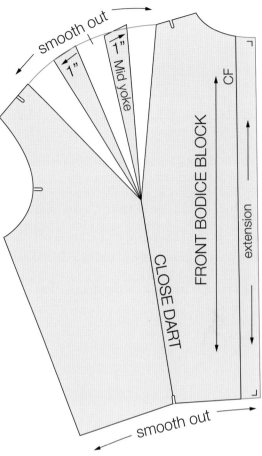

1. Draw a line parallel to the center front (CF) bodice to equal the diameter of your button plus ⅛ inch (3 mm). **Example: If you are using 5/8 inch (1.5 cm) buttons, your front extension will be ¾ inch (1.75 cm).**
2. Square off at neck and waist, as shown.
3. For gathers, draw three slash lines to apex (bust point): one from mid-yoke and two 1 inch (2.5 cm) out from mid-yoke.
4. Using slash-and-spread method, transfer dart to yoke line.
5. Cut slash lines to the edge of the apex.
6. Cut waist dart leg to the edge of the apex.

7. Close waist dart and tape shut.
8. Place pattern on to paper, spread slashed sections evenly, and secure.
9. Trace pattern, smoothing gathering line; use the center sections of the slash points as a guideline, as shown.
10. Smooth front waistline if needed, notching where front waist dart was closed.
11. Make a notch at the center of the gathers. **Note: You will be gathering the bodice between notches.**

Convertible collar

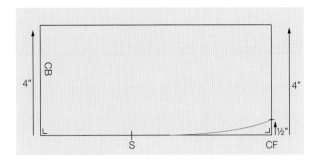 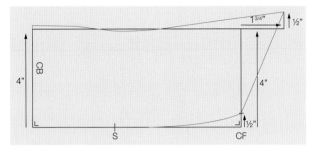

1. Draw a horizontal line equal to the front and back neckline measurement.
2. Mark center back (CB) and center front (CF).
3. Using back neckline measurement, mark shoulder (S).
4. Square a line 4 inches (10 cm) up from CB.
5. Square a line 4 inches (10 cm) up from CF and connect to CB.
6. Mark a point ½ inch (1.2 cm) up from CF line.

7. Draw a curved line (red curved line) using your French curve from S to this point.
8. Extend front collar edge 1¾ inches (4.25 cm) out from CF and ½ inch (1.2 cm) up. **Note: This will be the point of your collar.**
9. Redraw collar edge, connecting edge of collar and CF to point. Curve collar edge as shown. **Note: You can make the collar edge any shape you want.**

Sleeve with extended gathered cap

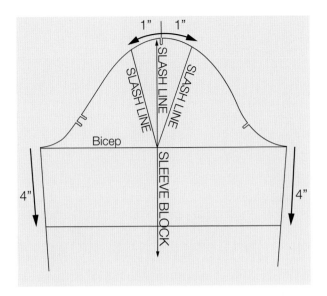
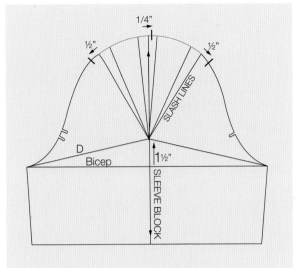

1. Trace basic sleeve 4 inches (10 cm) below bicep (you can make the sleeve any length you wish).
2. Draw slash lines down 2 inches (5 cm) away from center grain line to mid-bicep.
3. To extend the cap, slash down the center slash line (grain line), ending just before the bicep.
4. Also slash to-not-through bicep line from center grain line to underarm.
5. Raise bicep ½ inch (1.2 cm) and secure.
6. Slash two remaining lines using the slash-and-spread method

7. Spread sections evenly and secure.
8. Blend sleeve cap at gathers, as shown (red line).
9. Mark gathering notches ½ inch (1.2 cm) out from original slash lines. **Note: This will reduce the amount of ease for the sleeve cap in the non-gathering portion, as it is not necessary any more because of the gathers.**
10. Redraw center grain line and notch shoulder seam ¼ inch (6 mm) toward the front of the sleeve pattern. **Note: You will gather the sleeve into the yoke section of the bodice.**

Flared skirt

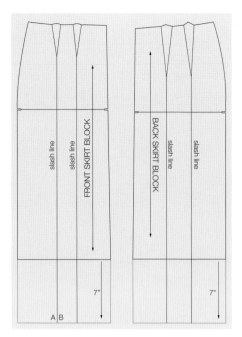

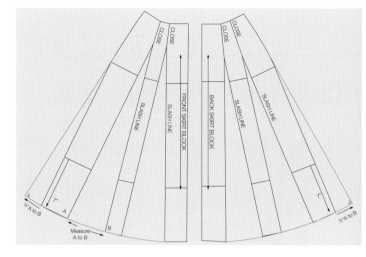

1. Trace front and back skirt blocks.
2. Extend length 7 inches (17.5 cm). **Note: You can extend the length as much or as little as you prefer.**
3. Draw slash lines from dart points to hem, parallel to CF and CB.
4. Label A and B on either side of slash line on the front pattern closest to the side-seam.
5. Transfer dart fullness to hem using the slash-and-spread method.

6. Measure the distance from A to B, and record_____.
7. Add half of this distance to both the front and the back side-seams.
8. Draw new side-seam, blending above the hipline, as shown, and squaring off at the hem.
9. Smooth out waist and hem if needed.

AUTHOR TIP

The side-seams may need to be balanced so the seam lies correctly; wait until the muslin fitting to determine this. If the seam pitches forward or backward, adjust the sweep of front or back skirt until the seam is vertical.

Muslin or Toile Fitting

- Before you draft the lining patterns, prepare a muslin for fit.
- Do not add seam allowance (SA) to pattern, as you will most likely be adjusting the muslin for fit.
- Draw the SA directly on to the muslin after tracing the working pattern.
- Make any necessary fit corrections to pattern.
- Now you can move on to the lining patterns.

> **AUTHOR TIP**
>
> You can either sew or pin muslin. I prefer to pin, as you can make quick adjustments to the fit of the garment on the dress form.

Figure 7.7A
Detail of muslin fit.

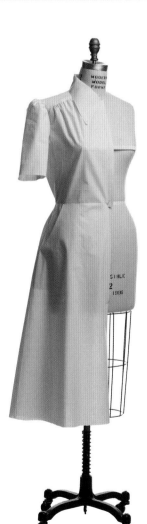

Figure 7.7
Checking muslin fit.

Completing the upper-collar and under-collar

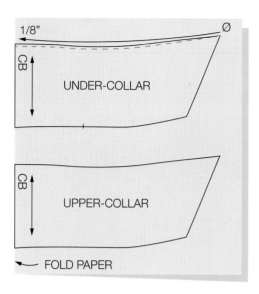

1/8"

∅

CB

UNDER-COLLAR

CB

UPPER-COLLAR

FOLD PAPER

1. Fold pattern paper in half and trace the collar twice—don't forget to mark your shoulder seam notch.
2. Label the first pattern as the upper collar.
3. On the second pattern, draft the under-collar by reducing the out-seam of the collar by ⅛ inch (3 mm) at the CB and blending to zero at the collar point (red dotted line).
4. Mark grain lines parallel to CB.

Front hip pocket directions

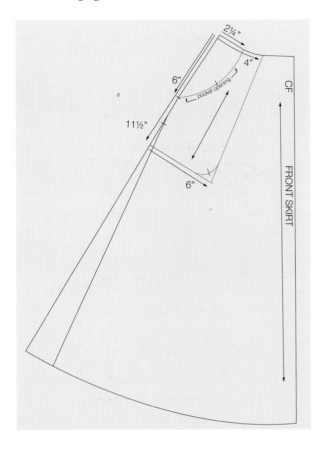

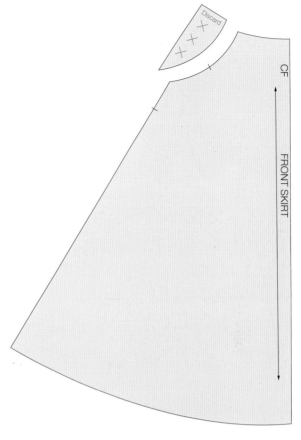

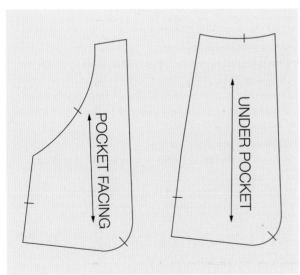

1. Copy front and back flared skirt and set aside for lining patterns.
2. You will draw the pocket opening and bag shape directly on to the skirt pattern. **Note: The pocket can be any shape you wish—just make sure that the pocket connects to the waistline and side-seam.**
3. For the pocket opening, measure 6 inches (15 cm) down from waist and 2¼ inches (5.6 cm) in from waist and mark.
4. Draw a curved line (red curve) connecting the points, and notch as shown.
5. For the pocket bag shape, measure 4 inches (10 cm) in from waist and mark.
6. Measure 11½ inches (13.75 cm) down from waist and square a line out 6 inches (15 cm).
7. Connect points as shown, curving the corner of the pocket bag, and notch (marked in red).
8. Mark grain line perpendicular to bottom pocket seam.
9. Trace the pocket shape twice.
10. Label one of the traced pocket shapes as the under-pocket.
11. Cut the pocket opening out for the second pocket shape, and label it as the pocket facing.
12. Cut out the pocket opening on the skirt and discard.
13. Make sure to transfer all markings to the pocket bags.

Front facing/lining

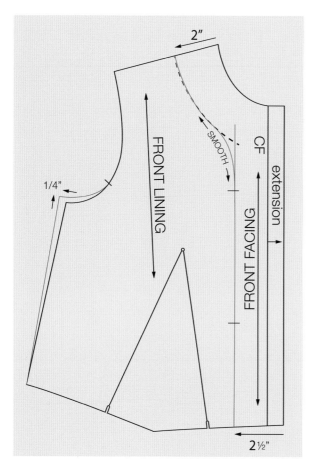

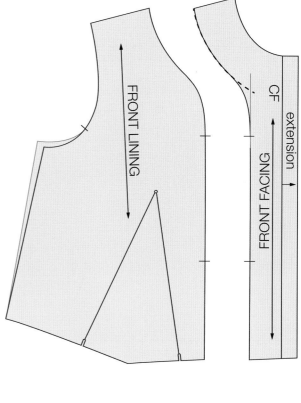

1. Trace front bodice block. **Note: As you only manipulated the darts and made no changes to the fit of the block, you do not need to use the manipulated pattern for the lining.**

2. Draw the front extension for the facing on the block, using the same front extension measurement you used for the bodice front (the diameter of the button plus ⅛ inch).

3. For the front facing, draw a parallel line (red line) 2½ inches (6.2 cm) in from the front extension.

4. Draw a curved line (red curved line) 2 inches (5 cm) in from neckline, and continue the curve until it meets the vertical line.

5. Smooth out as shown.

6. Mark two control notches for the sewing guide, as shown.

7. Starting at side-waistline, draw a line (red line) out and up ¼ inch (6 mm) to allow for ease in the lining pattern.

8. Blend to armhole notch.

9. Mark grain line for lining parallel to CF and cut apart.

10. Label front facing and front bodice lining.

Back bodice and sleeve linings

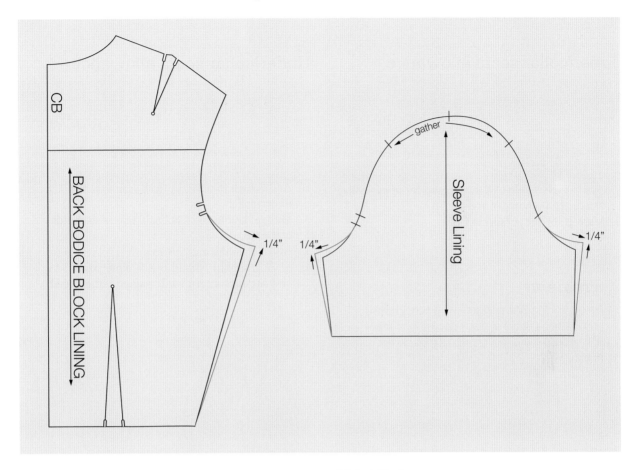

1. Trace the back bodice block and the shirtwaist sleeve pattern.
2. Starting at side-waistline on the back and the hem on the sleeve, draw a line (red line) out and up ¼ inch (6 mm) to allow for ease in the lining pattern.
3. Blend to armhole notches. **Note: You will gather the sleeve 2 inches (5 cm) on the front bodice armhole and 2½ inches (6.2 cm) on the back bodice arm-hole.**

Skirt linings

You have already traced the front and back skirt linings.

Production Pattern
Seam Allowances and Hems

Upper-collar seam allowance

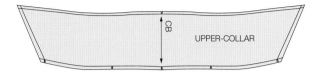

1. Add ¼ inch (6 mm) SA to all seams for upper-collar.
2. Notch at CB, shoulder, and the SA.
3. Mark grain line parallel to CB.

AUTHOR TIP

Before adding SAs and hems, be sure to walk your patterns and make any necessary corrections if seams and/or control notches do not match.

Under-collar seam allowance

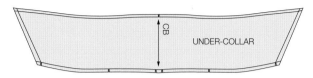

1. Add ¼ inch (6 mm) SA to all seams for the under-collar.
2. Make a double notch at back (one on each side of the CB).
3. Notch shoulder and the SA.
4. Mark grain line parallel to CB. **Note: Mark SAs and cut out pattern while paper is still folded!**

Front bodice, sleeve, and front facing seam allowances and hems

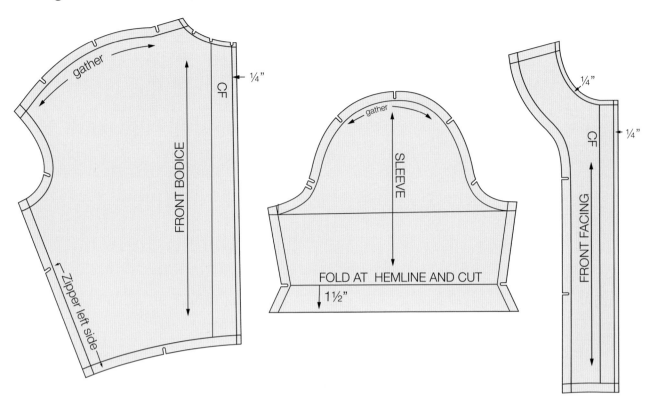

1. Add ¼ inch (6 mm) SA to back and front necklines and down CF.
2. Add ½ inch (1.2 cm) SA to remaining seams except sleeve hem.
3. The sleeve hem is 1½ inches (3.75 cm).
4. Notch 6 inches (15 cm) up on the left side of the bodice for zipper placement. **Note: As the dress has a fitted waist, you must have a side-zipper to be able to put the dress on.**

AUTHOR TIP

Make sure to fold paper back at hemline when cutting out, to ensure the hem lies correctly on garment.

Back bodice and yoke seam allowances

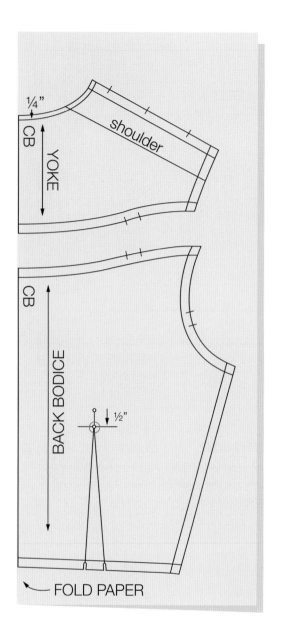

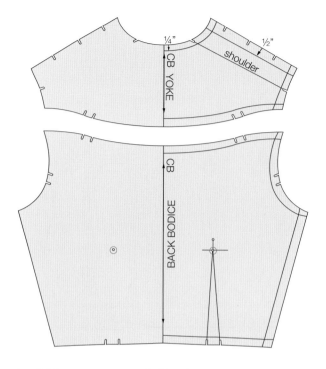

1. Fold pattern paper in half and trace the bodice back and yoke patterns.
2. Add ½ inch (1.2 cm) SA to all seams with the exception of the neckline.
3. Add ¼ inch (6 mm) SA to the neckline.

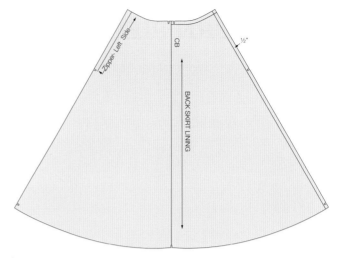

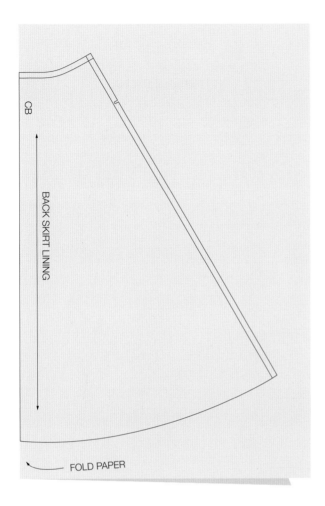

1. Fold pattern paper in half and trace the front and back skirt lining patterns.
2. Add ½ inch (1.2 cm) SA to all seams with the exception of the hems.
3. You do not add SAs to the hems as they are already "built in"; mark ½ inch (1.2 cm) up and notch.
4. Add a double notch on the CB waistline (one on each side) of the back skirt lining.

TECHNICAL FLATS AND FINISHED PATTERN PIECES

Technical flat front

Technical flat back

Self

1. Front bodice (cut 2).
2. Back bodice (cut 1).
3. Yoke (cut 2).
4. Sleeve (cut 2).
5. Upper-collar (cut 1).
6. Under-collar (cut 1).
7. Front skirt (cut 1).
8. Back skirt (cut 1).
9. Front facing (cut 2).
10. Under-pocket (cut 2).

Lining

1. Front bodice (cut 2).
2. Back bodice (cut 1).
3. Sleeve (cut 2).
4. Skirt front (cut 1).
5. Skirt back (cut 1).
6. Pocket facing (cut 2).

"In a machine age, dressmaking is one of the last refuges of the human, the personal, the inimitable."

Christian Dior

Figure 7.8
Front bodice detail.

The Coat Dress

Patterning concepts learned

- Portrait collar
- Double-breasted
- Classic princess style line with added fullness
- Inverted and knife pleats
- In-seam pocket
- Three-quarter one-piece sleeve with back seam

Figure 8.1
Designed coat dress.

The History of the Coat Dress

The coat dress is similar to the shirtwaist dress, but differs in that it has the styling of an overcoat and generally has long or dolman sleeves. While its distinguishing features mimic outerwear, it is meant to be worn indoors, and for decades has lent itself to a sophisticated, no-nonsense look. With its classic collar, lapels, and front fastenings, the coat dress has come to symbolize power dressing in its most glamorous form.

Historically, it is based on the eighteenth-century redingote, which is the French iteration of the English woman's riding coat—which, in turn, is a direct adaptation of the menswear version of the style. Initially the redingote was worn outdoors, and it was not until the 1820s, following the Empire period, that it developed into a close-fitting day-dress. This is when the dress took on its coat-like features and was cut with a collar and lapel. Sometimes the skirt opened up to show an underskirt. The redingote is also said to have its roots in the pelisse robe—an even earlier version of the coat dress which closed down the front with buttons, ribbons, or hidden closures.

The modern version of the coat dress is said to be inspired by the swagger coat, a popular outer garment defined by its pyramid shape, which first appeared in the early 1900s. A 1915 *Vogue* magazine article assured women that this new garment would become a staple in their wardrobes.

It was at this time, in the Edwardian period, that the stylish semi-formal version of the dress worn in single- or double-breasted versions and belted at the waist was identified as the coat-frock—once again a nod to the menswear influence.

Throughout the decades it continued to have a presence in fashion, and was particularly popular in the 1950s and 1960s. Diana, Princess of Wales, was known to favor coat dresses, which helped to maintain the style's popularity in the 1980s and 1990s. Keeping it in the family, the Duchess of Cambridge is often seen sporting the look. A possible reason why the coat dress is so popular with women in the royal family is that it serves a functional purpose as well as a stylish one: etiquette bars female members of the family from removing their outermost layer in public, viewing this as an "unladylike action."

The coat dress is often considered a more feminine version of the 1980s' "power suit" for women working in the corporate world. During this period women more than ever had positions of authority, and they adapted their wardrobe so as to look the part and be taken seriously. A popular saying of the time was "dress for success," and women looked to fashion to help them achieve it. A power suit conveyed a professional look that emulated menswear and helped women assert themselves in a male-dominated environment. The coat dress, which is a hybrid of both worlds, became a fashion staple.

Contemporary designers continue to love the look, and it is shown season after season. Modern versions are often being called a "blazer dress," a more masculine version of the coat dress but with the same sartorial elements. With its nod to menswear, it is a new form of power dressing that can transition easily from work to wherever your evening takes you.

Figure 8.2
Engraving of woman in pelisse, 1817.

Figure 8.3a
French woman wearing a spring coat dress, March 1946.

Figure 8.4
Contestant Joanna Clifton modeling a double-breasted mini coat dress for Grace Bros stores "Mannequin of the Year" fashion parade contest in Australia, 1970.

Figure 8.3b
The 'New Look' in coats, a tailored coat-dress with full skirt. *Housewife Magazine*, 1957.

Figure 8.5
Diana, Princess of Wales, wearing a tartan coat dress by Catherine Walker, 1990.

"In difficult times, fashion is always outrageous."

Elsa Schiaparelli

Contemporary Coat Dresses

Feminine and masculine versions of the coat dress are equally stunning on the runway.

Figure 8.6
Alexander McQueen, Runway, Paris Fashion Week, Fall/Winter 2019/2020.

Figure 8.7
Saint Laurent, Runway, Paris Fashion Week, Fall/Winter 2019/2020.

The Pattern
Start with the basic torso and sleeve blocks

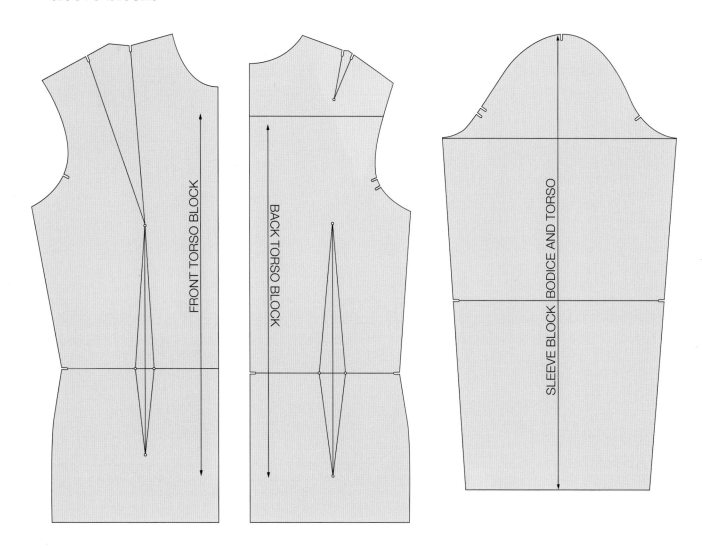

FRONT TORSO BLOCK

BACK TORSO BLOCK

SLEEVE BLOCK BODICE AND TORSO

Lengthen pattern, double breast development, and classic princess front

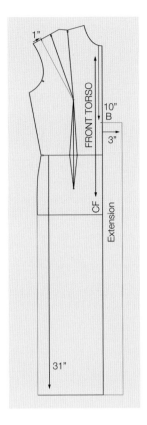
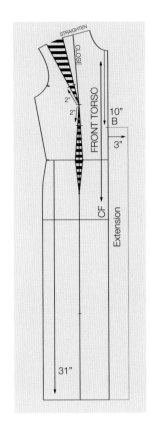
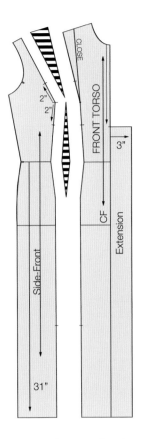

1. Trace front torso block, leaving enough space on paper for the front extension development.
2. Lengthen pattern 31 inches (77.5 cm) from waist. **Note: You can extend the length as much or as little as you prefer.**
3. Mark 10 inches (25 cm) down from center front (CF) neckline for collar depth, and label B. **Note: This is where the left and right sides overlap on the dress.**
4. Draw the extension 3 inches (7.5 cm) parallel to the CF line from B to hem. This makes it double-breasted.
5. Transfer shoulder dart to 1 inch (2.5 cm) from the shoulder seam using the slash-and-spread method.
6. Draw a slash line 1 inch (2.5 cm) from shoulder seam.
7. Cut slash line to the edge of the bust point (apex).
8. Cut shoulder dart leg to the edge of the bust point (apex).
9. Close shoulder dart and tape shut.
10. Mark control notches 2 inches (5 cm) from apex on all lines; notch apex.
11. Straighten shoulder seam if necessary.
12. Extend a line through center of contour dart to hem.
13. Mark control notch, as shown.
14. Cut front and side-front pieces apart, making sure to cut out the darts.
15. Smooth out the bust line if it looks too pointy or uneven.
16. Walk the pattern using an awl, starting at the waist; adjust pattern as needed to balance style line at shoulder and hemline.
17. Mark grain line on side-front perpendicular to waist.

Lengthen back pattern, shift shoulder dart, contour center back seam, classic princess back

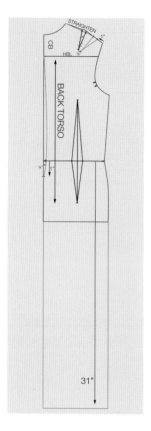
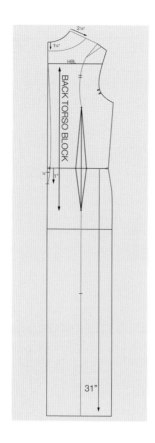
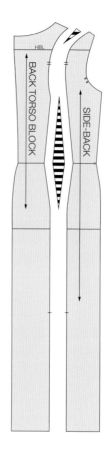

1. Curve center back (CB) seam ¼ inch (6 mm) in at waistline, and extend below waist 1 inch (2.5 cm). Draw a new CB line, blending to horizontal balance line (HBL).
2. Shift back neck dart to 1 inch (2.5 cm) from shoulder seam; shift dart point over ½ inch (1.2 cm). Straighten shoulder seam.
3. For back neckline, mark 2½ inches (6.2 cm) out from neckline and label D.
4. Square a line 1¼ inches (3 cm) down from CB neckline and draw a curved line to D with French curve. **Note: CB neckline should be parallel to CB; if it is not, adjust the depth of the back neckline.**
5. Measure back neckline and record _____.
6. Extend a line through center of contour dart to hem.
7. Mark control notch, as shown.
8. Starting at tip of shoulder dart, draw desired curve for princess line.

9. Mark a double notch, as shown. **Note: You must always have a double notch on back patterns.**
10. Cut back and side-back pieces apart, making sure to cut out the darts.
11. Smooth out any areas if they look too pointy or uneven.
12. Mark grain line on side-back perpendicular to waist.
13. Walk the pattern with an awl starting at the waist; adjust pattern as needed to balance style line at shoulder and hem.

Portrait collar development

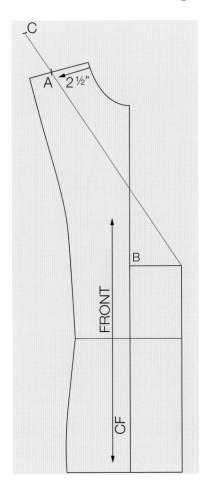
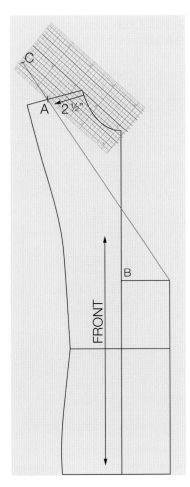
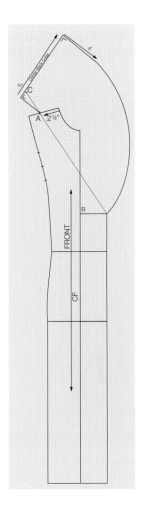

1. Trace front pattern, leaving enough space for portrait collar development.
2. Mark 2½ inches (6 cm) from high-point shoulder (HPS) and label A.
3. The back neckline measurement is A to C plus ⅛ inch (3 mm), so measure and record_____.
4. Draw a line from front edge of extension passing through A to C. This is the collar roll line. **Note: The point where the roll line passes through the CF is the depth of the portrait collar.**
5. Using the same back neck measurement, place ruler on A and draw a new line 1 inch (2.5 cm) to the left of C.
6. Square a line 10 inches (25 cm) from this mark, square a short line approximately 6 inches (15 cm) down from this mark, and draw a curved line to finish off the collar shape. Notch as shown.
7. Make sure to retain your CF line.

Adding flare to the front and side-front seams and side-seams, and inverted and back knife pleats to the side-back and back seams

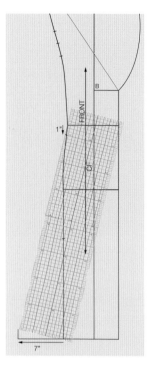 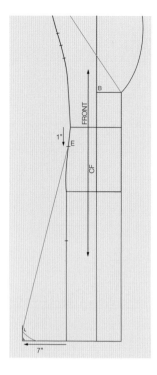 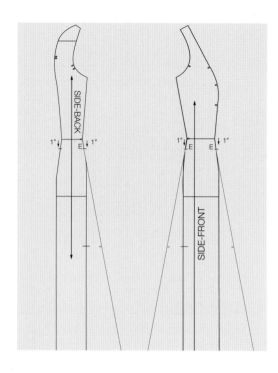

1. Trace front, side-front, and side-back patterns.
2. Extend hemline out 7 inches (17.5 cm), and square up as shown.
3. Mark 1 inch (2.5 cm) below waistline, and label E.
4. Measure the distance from E to hem, and record_____.
5. Using the recorded measurement, place the ruler on E and draw a new seam connecting it to the squared-off line at the hem.
6. Square the seam off until it meets up with the original hem.
7. Smooth out line if necessary.
8. Make the same pattern adjustments to seams, with the exception of the side-back seam as this will be developed into a knife pleat.

AUTHOR TIP

This new line appears shorter than the original because of the flare, but it is not. If you fail to adjust the new seam, the hemline will be uneven.

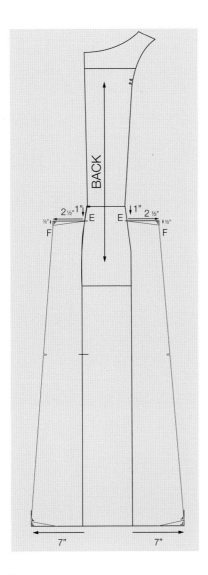

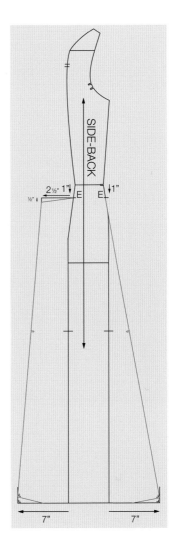

1. Trace back pattern.
2. Extend hemline out 7 inches (17.5 cm), and square up as shown.
3. Mark 1 inch (2.5 cm) below waistline on the side-back and CB seams, and label E.
4. Using the waistline as reference, square a line 2½ inches (6 cm) out from E.
5. Square down ½ inch (1.2 cm) and draw a slanted line; label F as shown.

6. Measure the distance from F to hem, and record_____.
7. Using the recorded measurement, place the ruler on F and draw a new line connecting it to the squared-off line at the hem.
8. Follow the same direction for the side-back seam.

Inverted pleat backing

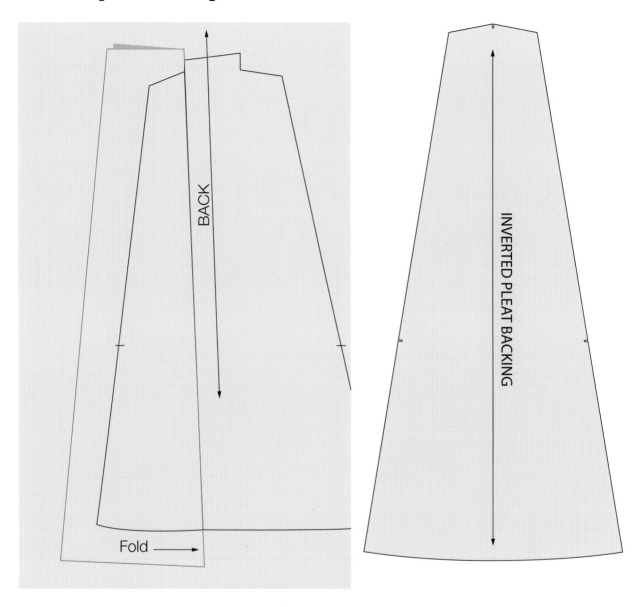

1. Use tracing paper to copy the inverted pleat for pleat backing.
2. Fold tracing paper in half.
3. Align the fold with the interior part of the pleat, trace, and cut out.
4. Mark grain line on the fold and notch as shown.
5. Trace another copy and set aside to use for lining development.

Three-quarter sleeve with back seam

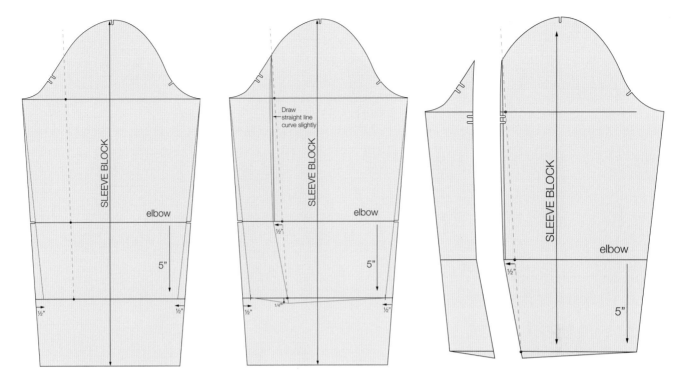

1. Trace sleeve block.
2. Mark hem 5 inches (12.5 cm) from elbow for three-quarter sleeves.
3. To narrow sleeve, mark ½ inch (1.2 cm) in at hem and draw new seam.

1. For back seam, find and mark the midpoint of the bicep, elbow, and wrist on the back of the sleeve and draw a line (dotted line).
2. Mark "a" ½ inch (1.2 cm) out from midpoint at elbow.
3. Mark "b" ¼ inch (6 mm) down from midpoint at hem.
4. Draw lines connecting the cross-marks and hem, as shown.
5. Cut sleeve into two pieces, as shown, cutting through the new back seam.

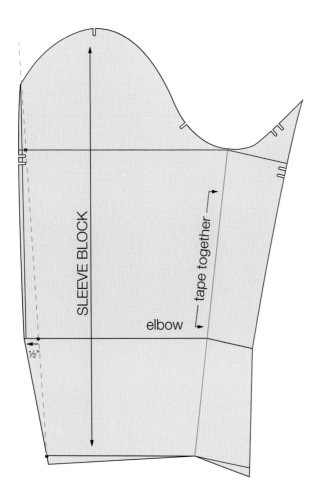

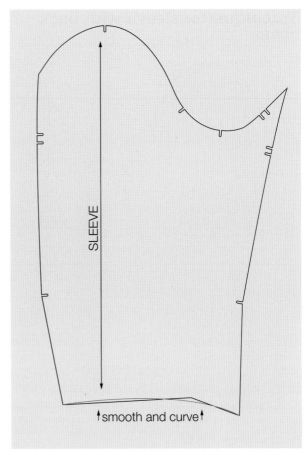

1. Tape the back portion of the original seam to the front.
2. Notch underarm where the two pieces were taped together.
3. Retain all notches, as shown.
4. Smooth out and slightly curve the hem.

Muslin or Toile Fitting

- Before you draft the lining patterns, prepare a muslin for fit.
- Do not add seam allowance (SA) to the pattern, as you will most likely be adjusting the muslin for fit.
- Draw the SA directly on to the muslin after tracing the working pattern.
- Make any necessary fit corrections to pattern.
- Now you can move on to the lining patterns.

> **AUTHOR TIP**
>
> Note: You can either sew or pin muslin. I chose to sew this muslin to ensure a proper fit of the garment on the dress form.

Figure 8.9
Detail of muslin fit.

Figure 8.8
Checking muslin fit.

Front facing

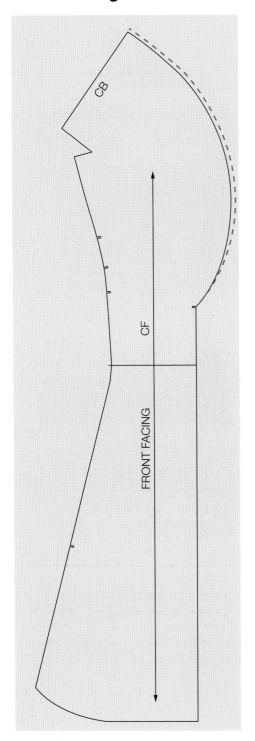

1. Trace front pattern.
2. Add ⅛ inch (3 mm), blending from breakpoint to edge of lapel at CB (red dotted line). **Note: This allows the lapel to be pressed under the ⅛ inch (3 mm), so the stitching line does not show on the garment.**

In-seam side pocket

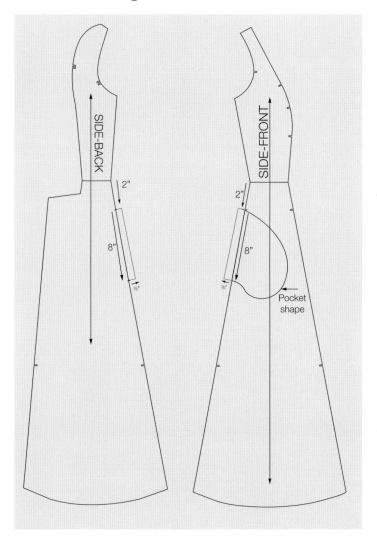

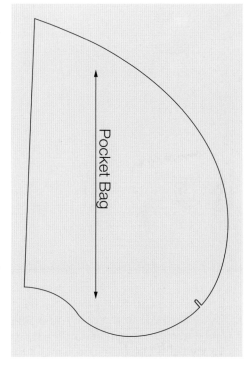

1. Trace side-front and side-back patterns, and set aside for lining development.
2. Mark pocket placement on both side-front and side-back patterns 2 inches (5 cm) down from waist on side-seams.
3. Mark pocket opening 8 inches (20 cm) down.
4. Extend the opening out ½ inch (1.2 cm). **Note: This will help to keep the pocket lining from showing.**
5. Draw desired shape of the pocket bag on front pattern piece. Do not include the pocket extension for the pocket bag.
6. Using a tracing wheel, trace a copy for the pocket bag pattern and notch as shown. **Note: I have ready-made stencils of basic pocket shapes to use when drafting them to save time and effort.**

Side-front and side-back lining

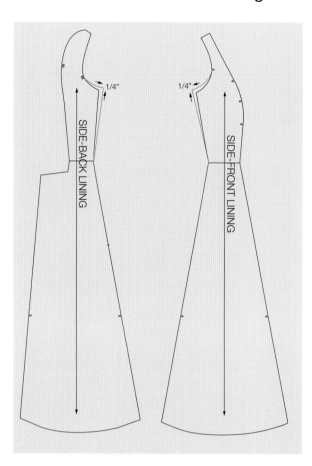

1. Using saved side-front and side-back pattern pieces and starting at the waistline, draw a line (red line) up and out ¼ inch (6 mm) to allow for ease in the lining pieces.
2. Blend (red curve) to armhole notches.

Back lining action pleat

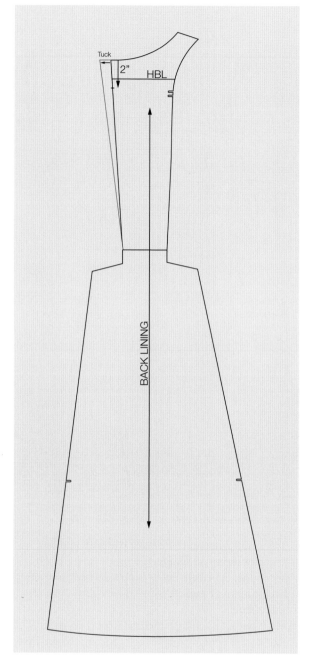

1. Trace back pattern.
2. Mark out 1 inch (2.5 cm) from CB and square down to HBL.
3. Continue line to meet waist.
4. At CB seam, mark 2 inches (5 cm) down for tuck.

Sleeve facing and lining

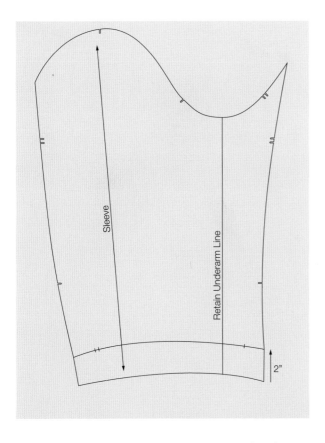

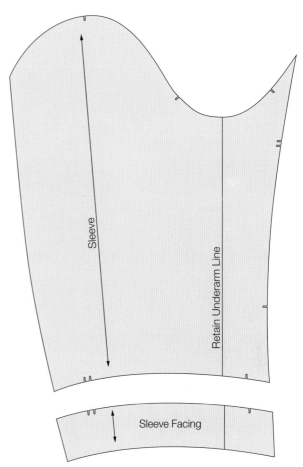

1. Trace sleeve pattern, retaining the original underarm line.
2. For sleeve facing, draw a parallel line 2 inches (5 cm) up from hem.
3. Notch as shown.
4. Cut out and set aside.

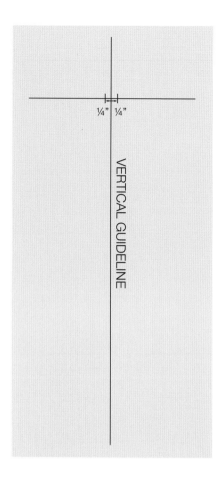

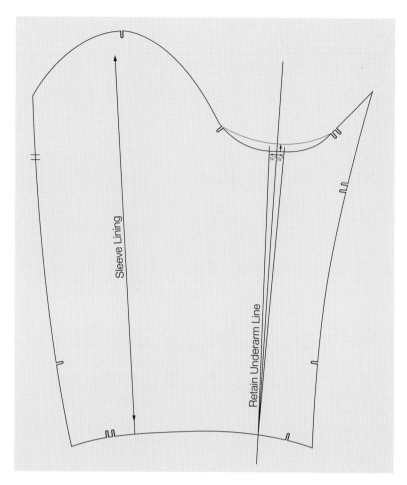

1. On paper, draw a vertical guideline; mark out ¼ inch (6 mm) on either side of the guideline.
2. For sleeve lining, slash the original underarm line down from underarm notch to hem, stopping just short of the edge.
3. Place side panel on the guideline and spread open to meet the marks, tape down, and trace pattern, retaining original grain line.
4. At new underarm notch, mark up ¼ inch (6 mm) and blend to notches. **Note: The guideline becomes your new underarm notch.**

Production Pattern
Seam Allowances and Hems

AUTHOR TIP

Before adding SAs and hems, be sure to walk
your patterns and make any necessary corrections if seams and/or control notches do not
match.

Front

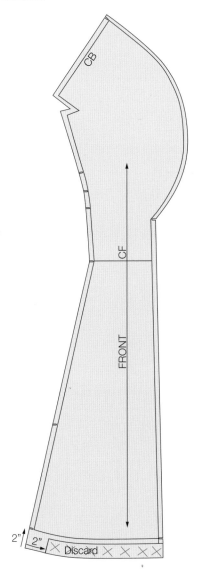

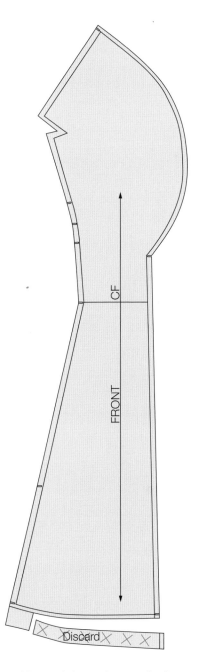

1. Trace front pattern.
2. Add ½ inch (1.2 cm) SA to all seams with the exception of the front, neckline, and hem.

3. Add ¼ inch (6 mm) SA to the front and neckline.
4. Mark hem 2 inches (5 cm); this includes the ½ inch
   (1.2 cm) SA.
5. Measure 1 inch (2.5 cm) in from side-seam and
   square down to hem.
6. Measure ½ inch (1.2 cm) down from original hem
   and draw line to squared line. **Note: You will discard this "wedge" when cutting out the pattern.**

Front facing seam allowance and hem

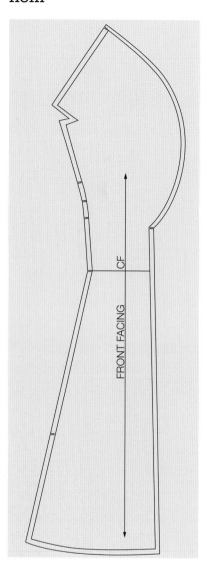

1. Add ¼ inch (6 mm) SA to front neckline and down CF.
2. Add ½ inch (1.2 cm) SA to all other seams.

Side-front, side-back, back, and inverted pleat backing seam allowances and hems

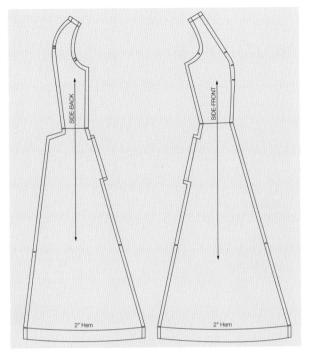

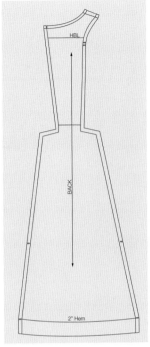

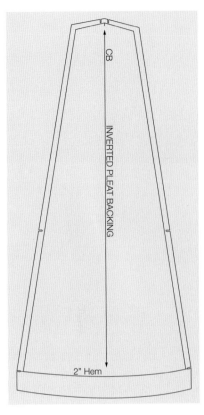

1. Add ½ inch (1.2 cm) SA to all seams with the exception of the back neckline and hems.
2. Add ¼ inch (6 mm) SA to back neckline.
3. Mark hems 2 inches (5 cm); this includes the ½ inch (1.2 cm) SA.

AUTHOR TIP

Make sure to fold paper back at hemline when cutting out to ensure the hem lies correctly on garment.

Sleeve and sleeve facing seam allowances and hems

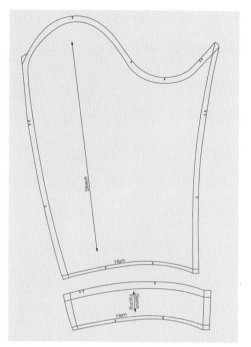

Side-front, side-back, back, inverted pleat backing, and pocket linings seam allowances and hems

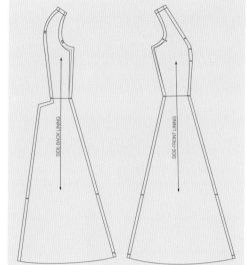

1. Add ½ inch (1.2 cm) SA to all seams with the exception of the hem.
2. Add ¼ inch (6 mm) SA to hems, as this is an enclosed seam.
3. Make sure to square off SA.

1. Add ½ inch (1.2 cm) SA to all seams with the exception of the back neckline and hem.
2. Add ¼ inch (6 mm) SA to the back neckline.
3. You do not add an SA to the hem, as it is already "built in"; mark and notch up ½ inch (1.2 cm).

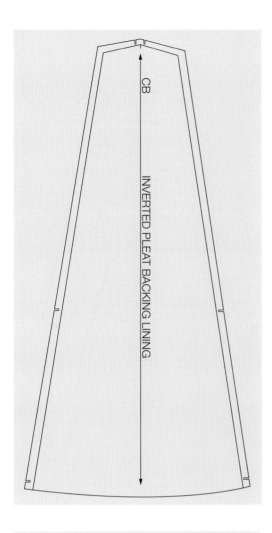

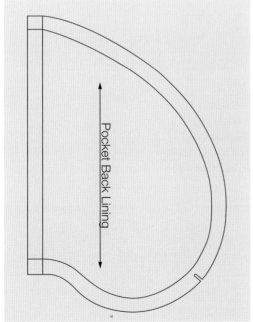

Sleeve lining seam allowance and hem

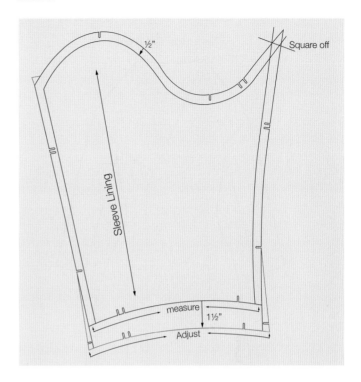

1. Extend sleeve lining length 1½ inches (3.75 cm) to allow for turnup and ease.
2. The lining will narrow at the hem, and needs to be adjusted so it will match the facing.
3. Measure the width of the original lining hem that will be sewn to the facing, and record_____.
4. Adjust the new hem's width to match the original measurement (red line).
5. Redraw sleeve seams to meet hem (red lines).
6. Make sure to square off SAs.
7. Retain all notches, and notch ½ inch (1.2 cm) up at hem.

TECHNICAL FLATS AND FINISHED PATTERN PIECES

Technical flat front

Technical flat back

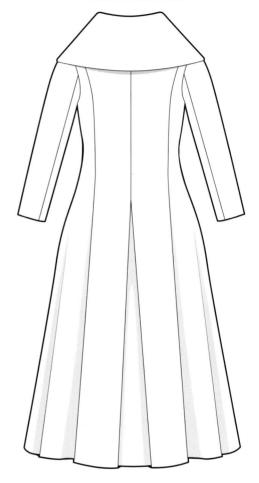

Self

1. Front (cut 2).
2. Side-front (cut 2).
3. Back (cut 2).
4. Side-back (cut 2).
5. Sleeve (cut 2).
6. Front facing (cut 2).
7. Sleeve facing (cut 2).
8. Inverted pleat backing (cut 1).

Lining

1. Back (cut 2).
2. Side-front (cut 2).
3. Side-back (cut 2).
4. Sleeve (cut 2).
5. Inverted pleat backing (cut 1).
6. Pocket bag (cut 4).

"Clothes aren't going to change the world. The women who wear them will."

Anne Klein

Portrait collar detail.

The Cheongsam

Patterning concepts learned

- Asymmetrical pattern
- Mandarin collar
- Front yoke with piping
- Cap sleeve with bias-bound hem
- French dart
- Pegged/pencil skirt with side-vent
- Lining patterns

Figure 9.1
Designed cheongsam.

The History of the Cheongsam

Forever identified with China, the cheongsam, also known as the *qi-pao*, is actually a blend of Chinese and Western clothing styles. It first appeared in the early twentieth century not long after the collapse of the Qing dynasty, and was adopted by Chinese women who wanted a more modern look in their clothing to complement their new-found political freedom

The figure-hugging, mandarin-collared dress with a daring side-slit that we identify as a cheongsam today was originally a looser fitting garment reminiscent of a long robe. The word *cheongsam* literally means "long robe" in Cantonese. It was not until the 1920s and 1930s, which are referred to as the "golden age" of the dress, that the cheongsam evolved into the current close-fitting version. In Shanghai and other urban areas the cheongsam was favored by female students and came to represent their youthful energy, which rivaled that of the flappers in the United States and England.

These young women, known as "social flowers," delighted in ballroom dancing, drinking, and socializing in nightclubs. They paraded around town in their cheongsams, which helped to cement the popularity of the dress.

With the onset of communism in 1949 the cheongsam fell out of favor in mainland China, and was later banned by the ruling party in 1966. But the style remained popular with women in Hong Kong, who continued to wear the dress throughout the 1950s and 1960s as a form of social resistance against the restrictions the communist government placed on clothing at the time. To this day, the cheongsam is still considered the national dress of Hong Kong.

The West has continually had a fascination with Eastern silhouettes. In the early 1900s designer Paul Poiret helped to popularize the chinoiserie style in the West, with a myriad of designers following his lead. Yves Saint Laurent's 1977–1978 couture collection was inspired by imperial Chinese themes, and featured heavily embroidered versions of the cheongsam along with other Eastern motifs.

The 1997 transfer of Hong Kong to China saw a resurgence of Asian influences, with many designers looking to the East for inspiration. The 1990 film *In the Mood for Love*, directed by Wong Kar-wai, furthered interest in the style. Set in 1960s' Hong Kong, it features Maggie Cheung and Tony Leung in a tragic story of unrequited love. Cheung is always dressed in exquisitely tailored cheongsams, which help to portray the film's dream-like aesthetic. More than 20 cheongsams are featured, and it is rumored that Hong Kong-based master-tailor Leung Ching-wah created some of the dresses for the film. Founded in 1966, his atelier, Linva Tailor, is one of the oldest cheongsam shops in Hong Kong, and still focuses on the craftmanship of the dress.

In the Mood for Love was not the first film to help popularize the dress. In the 1961 romantic drama *The World of Suzie Wong*, actress Nancy Kwan plays a lovable Hong Kong prostitute with a "heart of gold." The character dons body-hugging cheongsams in vibrant hues that were a typical silhouette of the time. Filmed in Hollywood, it has often been criticized for promoting the West's stereotypical viewpoint of the submissive Chinese woman. Nonetheless, the film helped to popularize the style outside China. At the same time a version of the cheongsam was adopted as the uniform of the food service industry in Hong Kong. The stigma of both eventually led to the cheongsam's fall in popularity in the following decades.

Today, designers with a Chinese heritage like Vivienne Tam and Anna Sui, along with the brand Shanghai Tang which opened in 1994 in Hong Kong, continue to broaden the popularity of the dress internationally. In Hong Kong and China the cheongsam is again popular for evening attire, and since the 1990s a red version of the dress has become a favored choice for brides on their wedding day.

In 2015 the Metropolitan Museum of Modern Art in New York mounted the exhibition "China: Through the Looking Glass," which explored the impact of Chinese aesthetics in the world of fashion. The exhibition was an in-depth study of how China has inspired modes of dress for centuries. The cheongsam's history aside, it is the elegant ease of the dress which has kept it a fashion mainstay that will continue well into the future.

> "To me, fashion is like a mirror. It's a reflection of the times. And if it doesn't reflect the times, it's not fashion."
>
> Anna Sui

Figure 9.2
Chinese "social flowers" in Westernized "cheongsams," 1937.

Figure 9.3
The World of Suzie Wong film promotion, 1960.

Figure 9.4
In the Mood for Love, starring Maggie Cheung and Tony Leung, 2000.

Figure 9.5
"China: Through the Looking Glass" display at the Metropolitan Museum of Art, New York, August 2015.

Contemporary Cheongsams

Modern twists on a timeless classic.

Figure 9.6
Huishan Zhang,
Runway, London
Fashion Week,
September 2019.

Figure 9.7
Huishan Zhang,
Runway, London
Fashion Week,
September 2019.

The Pattern

Start with front and back torso and
sleeve blocks

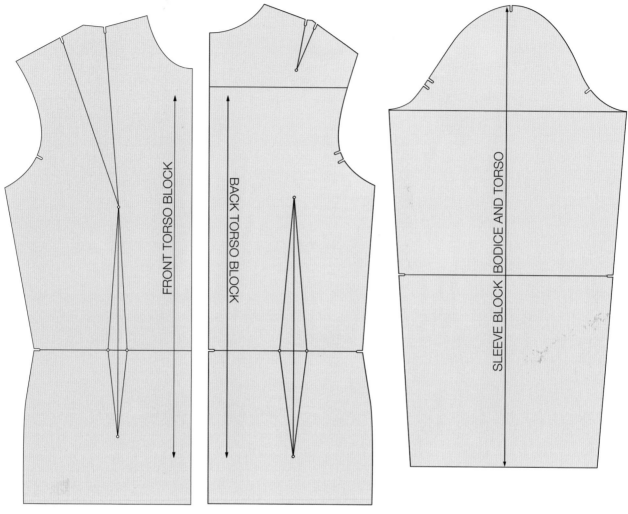

FRONT TORSO BLOCK

BACK TORSO BLOCK

SLEEVE BLOCK BODICE AND TORSO

French dart, lower neckline, and lower contour dart leg on front torso block

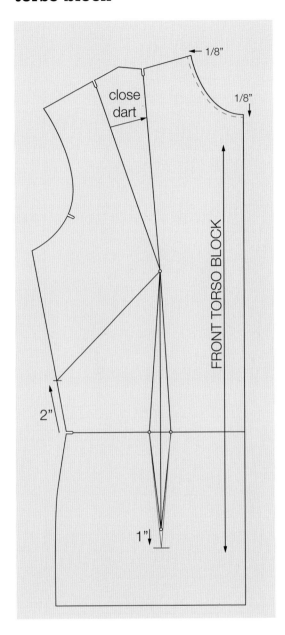

1. Trace front torso block.
2. Lower front neckline ⅛ inch (3 mm). **Note: We are opening up the neckline, as we are making the mandarin collar wider than usual and this will help with the fit.**
3. Transfer shoulder dart to side-seam by the slash-and-spread method to make a French dart.
4. Draw a line from apex (dart point) to side-seam 2 inches (5 cm) up from waistline.
5. Cut slash line from this line to apex.
6. Cut another slash line down dart leg on shoulder.
7. Close shoulder dart and tape shut.
8. Drop contour dart leg 1 inch (2.5 cm) and redraw dart.

Trueing dart legs

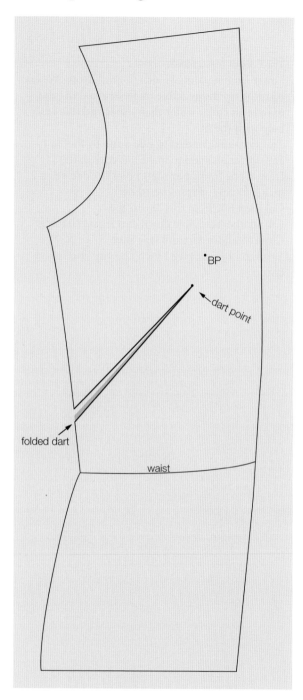

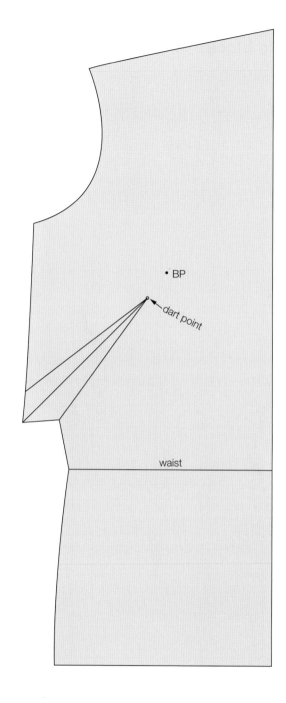

The excess (negative space) of the dart needs to match up with the seam so it will lie correctly when sewn. To do this you must fold the dart toward the waistline, closing the pattern as if you were sewing it. With the dart closed and folded, the pattern will be cut at the seamline.

1. Score the dart leg with an awl closest to the direction in which you are folding the dart.
2. To close the pattern, place the dart point (not the bust point!) on the side corner of the table matching up the dart legs, close, and tape down.
3. Cut the seam as if the dart is not there.
4. Open pattern up.

Lengthen and peg pattern, and mark dart points and skirt side-vent opening

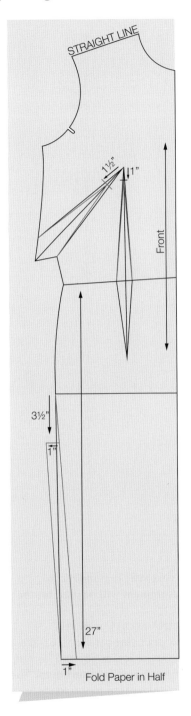

1. Fold a new piece of paper and trace new pattern on fold; straighten shoulder line if necessary.
2. Save initial pattern for lining development.
3. Mark French dart point 1½ inches (3.75 cm) from apex (bust point) and contour dart 1 inch (2.5 cm) from apex.
4. Draw new dart legs. **Note: You need to move the dart points away from the apex, so the darts don't look too pointy.**
5. Lengthen torso 27 inches (67.5 cm) from waist. **Note: You can extend the length as much or as little as you prefer.**
6. Taper skirt in 1 inch (2.5 cm) at hem, and redraw side-seam starting at the hip (red line).
7. For right side-vent, mark 3½ inches (8.75 cm) down from hipline.
8. Mark out 1 inch (2.5 cm) from new side-seam (red line) **Note: This creates a self-faced vent, which will also be mitered.**

Front yoke

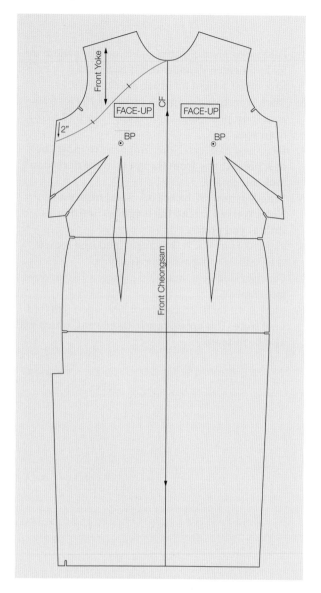

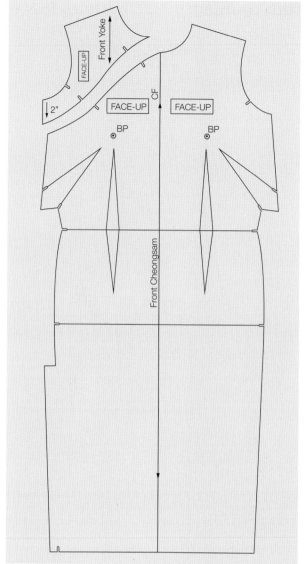

1. Cut pattern from paper, make sure to transfer all the markings with the exception of the side-slit to the folded side using an awl.
2. Open pattern and trace all markings to the left side of the pattern.
3. For front yoke, draw curved style line (red line) as shown from center front (CF) neckline to 2 inches (5 cm) below armhole.

4. Measure yoke style line and record_____. **Note: This measurement will be used for the piping on the yoke.**
5. Mark control notches, as shown.
6. Mark yoke grain line parallel to CF and cut apart.
7. Label patterns as indicated, with "face-up" on each pattern piece. **Note: You must mark "face-up" on asymmetrical pattern pieces to ensure the correct side of the fabric is cut out.**

Move back shoulder dart to armhole, lower neckline, and lower contour dart leg on back torso block

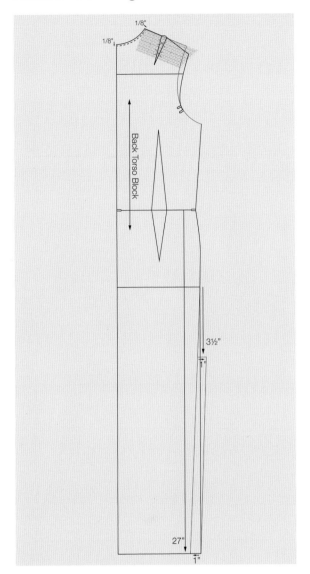

1. Trace back torso block.
2. To eliminate the shoulder dart, place ruler even with shoulder line at the neckline and draw a straight line.
3. Use the front shoulder measurement and mark the back shoulder to match.
4. True up armhole curve with French curve.
5. Lower neckline ⅛ inch (3 mm).
6. Lengthen torso 27 inches (67.5 cm) from waist.
7. Taper skirt in 1 inch (2.5 cm) at hem and redraw side-seam starting at the hip (red line).
8. For right side-vent, mark 3½ inches (8.75 cm) down from hip line.
9. Mark out 1 inch (2.5 cm) from new side-seam (red line).
10. Cut pattern out, flip pattern over, and trace; make sure to transfer all the markings with the exception of the side-slit.
11. Notch 9 inches (22.5 cm) down from waist at center back (CB) for zipper.
12. Label patterns as indicated, with "face-up" on each pattern piece.

Mandarin collar

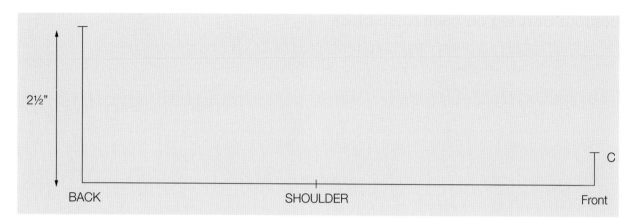

1. Measure front neckline and record_____.
2. Measure back neckline and record_____.
3. Draw a horizonal line equal to the front and back neckline measurements.
4. Mark CB and center front (CF).
5. Using back neckline measurement mark shoulder.
6. Square a line 2½ inches (6.2 cm) up from CB.
7. Square up ½ inch (1.2 cm) from CF and label as point C.

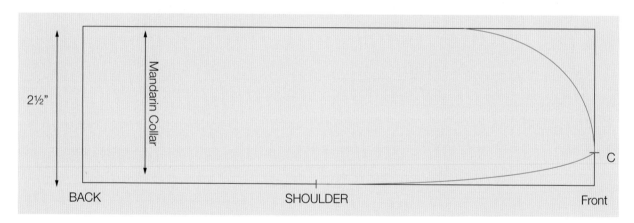

1. Draw a curved line (red line) from shoulder mark to C.
2. Square a line 2½ inches (6.2 cm) up from C.
3. Draw a line parallel to the neckline from the CB to the CF.
4. Curve front neckline, as shown, to complete the collar edge.
5. Mark grain line parallel to the CB.

Cap sleeve

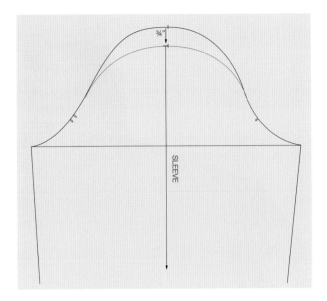

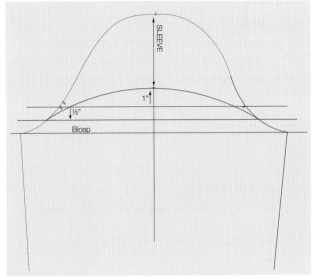

1. Trace top of sleeve.
2. To reduce cap ease, lower cap ¾ inch (1.75 cm) and blend as shown; mark shoulder notch ¼ inch (6 mm) in from center of sleeve (the grain line is usually the center).
3. Draw a parallel line up from bicep, landing ½ inch (1.2 cm) below control notches.

4. Mark up 1 inch (2.5 cm) more at center of sleeve and draw a curved line for edge of sleeve, as shown (red line). **Note: You can adjust the shape and size of the cap sleeve if desired.**
5. Measure new sleeve hem, bicep to bicep, and record _____. **Note: This measurement will be used for the bias-bound hem.**

Muslin or Toile Fitting

- Before you draft the lining patterns, prepare a muslin for fit.
- Do not add seam allowance (SA) to pattern, as you will most likely be adjusting the muslin for fit.
- Draw the SA directly on to the muslin after tracing the working pattern.
- Make any necessary fit corrections to pattern.
- Now you can move on to the lining patterns.

> **AUTHOR TIP**
>
> Note: You can either sew or pin muslin. I prefer to pin, as you can make quick adjustments to the fit of the garment on the dress form.

Figure 9.8A
Detail of muslin fit.

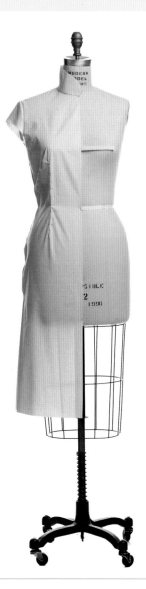

Figure 9.8
Checking muslin fit.

Left and right back seam allowances and hems

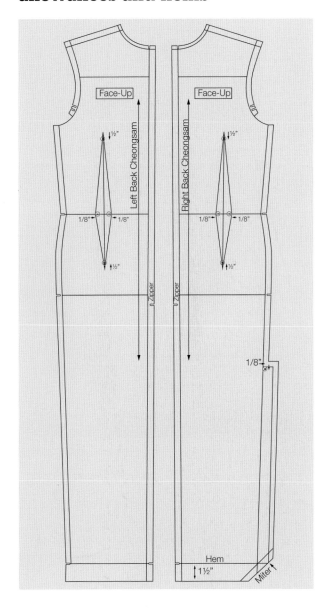

1. Trace left and right back patterns.
2. Circle and drill vertical dart points ½ inch (1.2 cm) into the dart and horizontal dart points ⅛ inch (3 mm) into the dart.
3. Circle and drill into vent ⅛ inch (3 mm) in as shown.
4. Add ½ inch (1.2 cm) SA to all seams with the exception of the back neckline and the armhole.
5. Add ¼ inch (6 mm) SA in the back neckline.
6. For armhole, mark ½ inch (1.2 cm) down from notch and square out ½ inch (1.2 cm) for the SA.
7. Continue SA up to shoulder, as shown. **Note: You do not need an SA for the rest of the armhole as it is bias bound.**
8. Add 1½ inches (3.75 cm) for hem.
9. To miter back vent, follow the directions for the front pattern.
10. Add ½ inch (1.2 cm) SA to the mitered edge.

Front yoke seam allowance

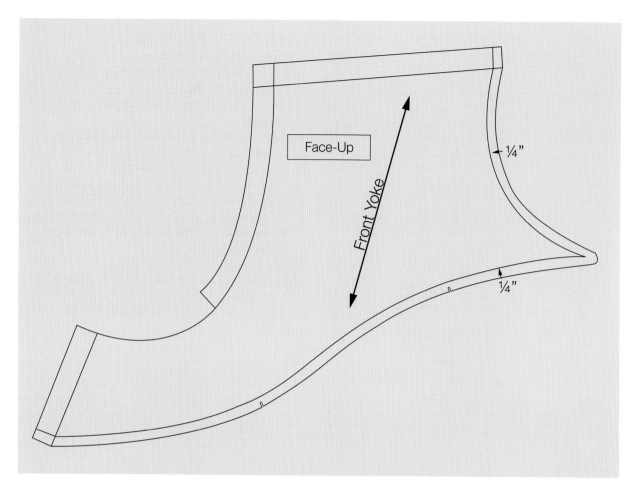

1. Add ¼ inch (6 mm) SA to front neckline and front yoke style line.
2. Add ½ inch (1.2 cm) SA to shoulder and side-seam.
3. For armhole, mark ½ inch (1.2 cm) down from notch and square out ½ inch (1.2 cm) for SA.
4. Continue SA up to shoulder, as shown.

Mandarin collar seam allowance

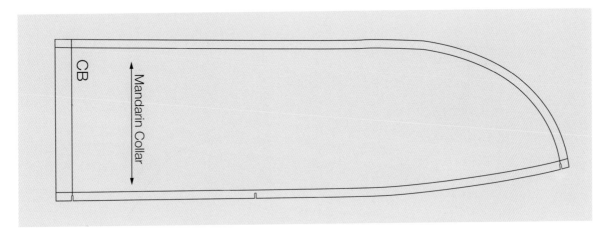

1. Add ¼ inch (6 mm) SA to neckline and edge of collar.
2. Add ½ inch (1.2 cm) SA to CB.

Sleeve and sleeve lining seam allowances

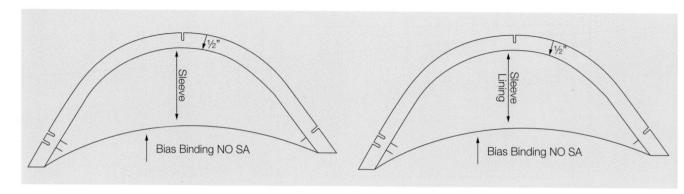

1. Add ½ inch (1.2 cm) SA to sleeve cap.
2. No SA is added to the hem, as it is bias bound. **Note: Both the sleeve shell and lining are identical, so, depending on the weight of your fabric, you can cut the lining in either fabric.**

Front and back seam allowances and hems

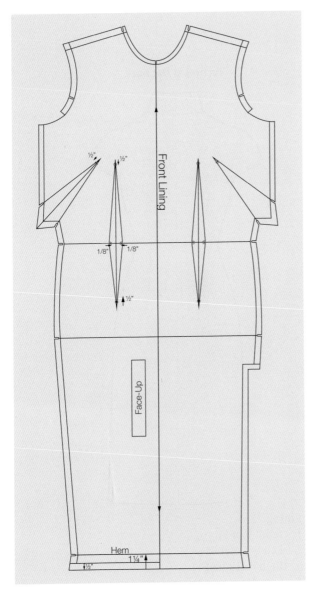

1. Trace front and back linings.
2. Circle and drill vertical dart points ½ inch (1.2 cm) into the dart and horizontal dart points ⅛ inch (3 mm) into the dart.
3. Add ½ inch (1.2 cm) SA to shoulder seams and side-seams.
4. Add ¼ inch (6 mm) SA to front and back necklines.
5. For armhole, mark ½ inch (1.2 cm) down from notch and square out ½ inch (1.2 cm) for SA.
6. Continue SA up to shoulder, as shown.
7. Add ½ inch (1.2 cm) to hemline.
8. Notch up 1¼ inches (3 cm) for hem. **Note: You only need to add the ½ inch (1.2 cm) to the hemline for the lining to hang properly inside the dress.**

TECHNICAL FLATS AND FINISHED PATTERN PIECES

Technical flat front

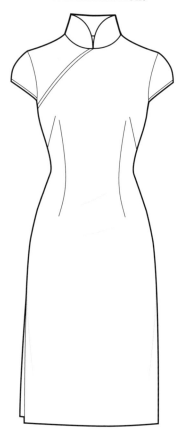

Technical flat back

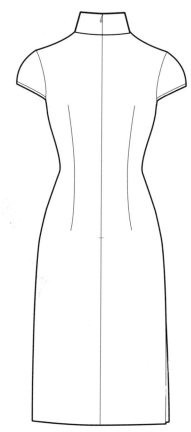

Self
1. Front (cut 1).
2. Front yoke (cut 1).
3. Left back (cut 1).
4. Right back (cut 1).
5. Mandarin collar (cut 2).
6. Cap sleeve (cut 2).
7. Sleeve hem bias binding (cut 2).
8. Yoke piping (cut 1).

Lining
1. Front (cut 1).
2. Left back (cut 1).
3. Right back (cut 1).
4. Cap sleeve (cut 2).

"Elegance is elimination."

Cristóbal Balenciaga

Figure 9.9
Bodice detail.

Glossary

Action pleat: Pleat located at the center back of the lining in a jacket that allows for ease of movement.

Apex: The bust point.

Armhole princess style line: A dart-equivalent seam that starts in the armhole of a garment.

Armscye: The armhole.

Bias: A diagonal line 45 degrees to the straight and cross-grain of a fabric.

Block: A basic pattern (also called a sloper) representing the shape of the body, from which other patterns are derived.

Breakpoint: The location at the front of the jacket where the lapel folds back; this is the start of the roll line.

Classic princess style line: A dart-equivalent seam that starts at the shoulder of a garment.

Collar: The part of a garment that finishes off the neckline.

Collar stand: The section of the collar that raises the collar off the neck.

Control notch: Notches indicating where seams match in a garment; they are the "road-map" to reading a pattern.

Dart: A shape, usually triangular, on a pattern used to take away excess fabric in order to fit the contour of the body.

Depth: The location on the lapel of a garment where the fabric overlaps.

Drill point/hole: The reference point used in pattern-making for dart, pocket, buttonhole, tuck, and vent placement. In industry the drill hole is always marked inside the finished seam to cover the markings on the finished garment.

Ease: Extra measure at key points (sleeve, back, shoulder, and bust) added for comfort and movement.

Face: The correct side of fabric.

Face-up: In patternmaking, you will write "face-up" on the pattern to indicate placing the fabric with the correct side facing up when you cut it out.

Facing: A layer of fabric sewn to the edge of a garment to finish it.

French tack: See Swing tack.

Front extension: The extra width on the front of a pattern needed for the addition of buttons and button-holes.

Gather: To reduce fabric fullness in a garment on a line of stitching.

Gorge line: Seam line where the collar and the lapel join.

Grain line: The line which indicates the direction of the grain on a pattern. Patterns are usually placed on the straight grain (warp).

High point shoulder: The location where the shoulder meets the neckline.

Interfacing: A support fabric either sewn in or fused on, and used for stabilizing an area of a garment.

Lining: A lightweight fabric constructed in the shape of the garment, and used to finish and protect the inside of the garment.

Muslin: A cotton fabric used to make a mock-up of the garment for fitting purposes; the actual sample is called either a "muslin" or a "toile."

Notch: See "Control notch."

Placket: Finishing for an opening; can be cut on the bias or on the straight grain.

Pleat: Fabric that has been folded over itself, used for fitting and to manipulate fullness.

Production pattern: The final, corrected pattern. This is the only pattern which has seam allowances and hems drawn on it.

Roll line: The line where the lapel or collar turns and folds back towards the body

Seam allowance (SA): The area between the seam line and the cutting line of the fabric.

Self: In patternmaking, "self" indicates fashion fabric.

Slash-and-spread: Technique in patternmaking where you cut and spread the pattern to create fullness.

Sleeve cap: The top part of the sleeve.

Style line: A seam line on a garment used to create a visual effect.

Sweep: The width of the garment's hemline.

Swing tack: A thread chain made by hand crocheting a chain-stitch, used to hold two or more layers loosely together.

Tack: To sew two pieces of fabric together with thread temporarily. Typically intended to be removed, tacking stitches are also used to secure the lining permanently to the outer garment.

Technical flat: The technical drawing used in the fashion industry to show the design details of a garment.

Toile: See "Muslin."

Truing-up a seam: The process of checking and correcting seam lines in a pattern to ensure they match up.

Tuck: A fold or pleat that has been stitched down.

Vent: An opening used in the hems of jackets and skirts to allow for ease of movement.

Walking a seam: Truing-up a seam by placing the seamlines of two patterns together and matching them lengthwise to ensure they are equal.

Bibliography

Becker, A. "The Body." *A Cultural History of Dress and Fashion in the Age of Empire.* London: Bloomsbury Academic, 2017.

Bourhis, K. *The Age of Napoleon: Costume from Revolution to Empire, 1789–1815.* New York: Metropolitan Museum of Art, 1989.

Bradshaw, J. *Dreams That Money Can Buy: The Tragic Life of Libby Holman.* New York: William Morrow, 1985.

Chrisman-Campbell, K. "France." *Berg Encyclopedia of World Dress and Fashion: West Europe.* Ed. Lise Skov. Oxford: Berg, 2010. *Bloomsbury Fashion Central.* Available online: http://dx.doi.org.proxy.artic.edu/10.2752/BEWDF/EDch8036a (accessed November 5, 2019).

CNN Style, "Sexy, skintight, sophisticated: How China's iconic dress has survived a century." 2015. Available online: https://www.cnn.com/style/article/cheongsam-exhibition-hk/ (accessed June 18, 2019).

Cunningham, P. "Television." *Berg Encyclopedia of World Dress and Fashion: The United States and Canada.* Ed. Phyllis G. Tortora. Oxford: Bloomsbury Academic, 2010.

Da Cruz, E. "Cocktail dress." The *Berg Companion to Fashion.* Ed. Valerie Steele. Oxford: Bloomsbury Academic, 2010, *Bloomsbury Fashion Central.* Available online: http://dx.doi.org.proxy.artic.edu/10.5040/9781474264716.0003345 (accessed May 5, 2019).

DeLong, M. "Fashion, Theories of." *The Berg Companion to Fashion.* Ed. Valerie Steele. Oxford: Bloomsbury Academic, 2010, *Bloomsbury Fashion Central.* Available online: http://dx.doi.org.proxy.artic.edu/10.5040/9781474264716.0007020 (accessed November 11, 2019).

De Osma, G. *Fortuny: The Life and Work of Mariano Fortuny.* New York: Rizzoli, 1994.

Diliberto, G. *Debutante: The Story of Brenda Frazier.* New York: Knopf, 1987.

Drake, N. ed. *The Sixties: A Decade in Vogue.* New York: Prentice Hall Press, 1988.

Garrett, V. "Overview: Hong Kong." *Berg Encyclopedia of World Dress and Fashion: East Asia.* Ed. John E. Vollmer. Oxford: Berg Publishers, 2010, [online]. Available online: http://dx.doi.org.proxy.artic.edu/10.2752/BEWDF/EDch6024 (accessed October 31, 2019).

Gross E. and F. Rottman. *Halston: An American Original.* New York: HarperCollins Publishers, Inc., 1999.

Hough, R. *Edward and Alexandra: Their Private and Public Lives.* London: St. Martin's Press, 1993.

Lance, J. "This is why Kate Middleton isn't allowed to take her coat off in public," *Glamour.* 2018. Available online: https://www.glamour.com/story/this-is-why-kate-middleton-isnt-allowed-to-take-off-her-coat (accessed November 1, 2019).

Lee, C. "Chinese dress in Singapore." *Berg Encyclopedia of World Dress and Fashion: South Asia and Southeast Asia.* Ed. Jasleen Dhamija. Oxford: Bloomsbury Academic, 2010. *Bloomsbury Fashion Central.* Available online: http://dx.doi.org.proxy.artic.edu/10.2752/BEWDF/EDch4061 (accessed October 31, 2019).

Lee, S. *American Fashion: The Life and Lines of Adrian, Mainbocher, McCardell, Norell, and Trigère.* New York: Quadrangle/New York Times Book Co., 1975.

McCardell, C. *What Shall I Wear?: The What, Where, When, and How Much of Fashion.* New York: Simon & Schuster, 1956.

Miller, E. *Balenciaga.* London: V&A Publications, 2007.

PBS. "What is a shirtwaist?," *The American Experience.* 2019. Available online: https://www.pbs.org/wgbh/americanexperience/features/triangle-fire-what-shirtwaist/ (accessed November 5, 2019).

Rubenstein, H. *100 Unforgettable Dresses.* New York: Harper Design, 2012.

Steele V. *Women of Fashion: Twentieth Century Designers.* New York: Rizzoli International, 1991.

Talley, A. *Diane von Furstenberg: The Wrap.* New York: Assouline, 2004.

Tortora, P. and K. Eubank. *Survey of Historic Costume,* fifth edition. New York: Fairchild Books, 2010.

Tortora, P. and S. Keiser. *The Fairchild Books Dictionary of Fashion,* fourth edition. London: Bloomsbury Publishing, 2014.

Tulloch, C. Bloomsbury Fashion Central, "'We also should walk in the newness of life': Individualized Harlem style of the 1930s." *The Birth of Cool: Style Narratives of the African Diaspora.* London: Bloomsbury Academic, 2018, *Bloomsbury Fashion Central.* Available online: http://dx.doi.org.proxy.artic.edu/10.5040/9781474262880.ch-002 (accessed November 9, 2019).

Vaughan, H. "Icon: Tracing the path of the 1950s' shirtwaist dress," *Journal of American Culture, Special Issue: Fashion.* Vol 32, No. 1, March 2009.

Victoria and Albert Museum. Available online: https://www.vam.ac.uk/articles/biba (accessed August 6, 2019).

Von Furstenberg, D. and L. Francke. *Diane: A Signature Life.* New York: Simon & Schuster, 1998.

Ward, S. "A-line dress." *The Berg Companion to Fashion.* Ed. Valerie Steele. Oxford: Bloomsbury Academic, 2010, *Bloomsbury Fashion Central.* Available online: http://dx.doi.org.proxy.artic.edu/10.5040/9781474264716.0000480 (accessed October 24, 2019).

Warner, P. "The Americanization of fashion: Sportswear, the movies and the 1930s." *Twentieth-Century American*

Fashion. Ed. Linda Welters and Patricia A. Cunningham. Oxford: Berg, 2008.

Wellington, E. "The all-American shirtwaist dress: A longtime style gets a practical, flattering update." *Chicago Tribune*, September 4, 2016. Available online: http://proxy.artic.edu/login?url=https://search-proquest-com.proxy.artic.edu/docview/1816426499?accountid=26320 (accessed November 10, 2019).

Wu, J. *Chinese Fashion: From Mao to Now*. London: Bloomsbury Academic, 2009.

Recommended Reading

Burnham, D.K. *Cut My Cote*. Ontario: Royal Ontario Museum, 1997.

Carr, R. *Couture: The Art of Fine Sewing*. Portland, ON: Palmer/Pletsch Publishing, 1993.

Duburg, A. and R. Van der Tol. *Draping: Art and Craftsmanship in Fashion Design*. Netherlands: De Jonge Hond, 2009.

Joseph-Armstrong, H. *Patternmaking for Fashion Design*. New York: Prentice Hall, 2009.

Nakamichi, T. *Pattern Magic*. London: Laurence King, 2010.

Powell, P. *Tailored Fashion Design*, New York: Fairchild Books, 2011.

Rissanen, T. and H. McQuillan. *Zero Waste Fashion Design*. New York: Fairchild Books, 2016.

Sato, S. *Transformational Reconstruction*. St. Helena: Center for Pattern Design, 2011.

Shaeffer, C. *Couture Sewing Techniques*. Newtown, CT: Taunton Press, 2001.

Shaeffer, C. *Fabric Sewing Guide*. Cincinnati, OH: Krause Publications, 2008.

Acknowledgments and Image Credits

Acknowledgments

After the success of my first patternmaking book on jacket and coat design, I decided to continue with a follow-up on iconic dress designs. I was again fortunate to have my friend and colleague Sharon Shoji's support. Sharon offered vital feedback, and graciously edited my copy in all phases of the manuscript.

Special thanks also go to photographers Scott Shigley, who through the years has always made my designs look incredible, and John Boehm, who came along for the ride on this shoot.

This book is dedicated to my parents.

Image Credits

Cover: Photo by Scott Shigley and John Boehm.
Dress photography: Scott Shigley and John Boehm.
Technical drawings and flats: Author.
P3: Photo by Scott Shigley and John Boehm.
P7: Photo by Scott Shigley.
P9: Photo by Pamela Vanderlinde.

Chapter 1

Ch1.2 *Portrait of Josephine as Venus* by Andrea Appiani, 1796, {{PD-US}}, available online: https://commons.wikimedia.org/wiki/File:Jos%C3%A9phine_as_Venus_by_Andrea_Appiani.png.
Ch1.3 Postcard, c. 1911, {{PD-US}}, available online: https://commons.wikimedia.org/wiki/File:HobbleSkirtPostcard.jpg.
Ch1.4 Source Museo del Traje, https://creativecommons.org/licenses/by-sa/4.0/deed.en, available online: https://commons.wikimedia.org/wiki/File:Museo_del_Traje_-_MT111885_-_Vestido_Delphos.jpg.
Ch1.5 Photo by Frank Wolfe, Lyndon B. Johnson Library, {{PD-US}}, available online: https://commons.wikimedia.org/wiki/File:Vietnam_War_protestors_at_the_March_on_the_Pentagon.jpg.
Ch1.6 Molly Goddard, Runway, London Fashion Week, February 2019, photo by Jack Taylor/BFC/Getty Images.
Ch1.7 Gucci, Runway, Milan Fashion Week Spring/Summer 2020, photo by John Philips/Getty Images.

Chapter 2

Ch2.2 Image courtesy of Metropolitan Museum of Art, New York, item #LC-65_119_EGDP024371.
Ch2.3 Photo by W. & D. Downey, London, via Wikimedia Commons, {{PD-US}}, available online: https://commons.wikimedia.org/wiki/File:Alexandra_of_Denmark02.jpg.
Ch2.4 Photo by Bettmann/Getty Images.
Ch2.5 Photo by Hulton Archive/Getty Images.
Ch2.6 Slava Zaitsev Fashion Laboratory, Mercedes-Benz Fashion Week, Autumn/Winter 2019/2020, Photo by Oleg Nikishin/Getty Images.
Ch2.7 Alexander McQueen, Runway, Paris Fashion Week, Fall/Winter 2018/2019, photo by Kristy Sparow/Getty Images.

Chapter 3

Ch3.2 George Grantham Bain Collection, Library of Congress, reproduction number LC-DIG-ggbain-12393, available online: https://commons.wikimedia.org/wiki/File:Violet_Romer_in_flapper_dress,_LC-DIG-ggbain-12393.jpg.
Ch3.3 Photo by Jac. de Nijs/Anefo, https://www.nationaalarchief.nl/onderzoeken/fotocollectie/ab08cfb0-d0b4-102d-bcf8-003048976d84, https://creativecommons.org/licenses/by-sa/3.0/nl/deed.en, available online: https://commons.wikimedia.org/wiki/File:Mary_Quant_in_a_minidress_(1966).jpg.
Ch3.4 Eric Koch/Anefo, CC0 1.0 Universal Public Domain Dedication, available online: https://commons.wikimedia.org/wiki/File:Mondriaanmode_door_Yves_Saint_Laurent_(1966).jpg.
Ch3.5 Photo by Vernon Merritt III/The LIFE Picture Collection/Getty Images.
Ch3.6 Courrèges, Runway, Paris Fashion Week, Fall/Winter 2019/2020, photo by Victor Virgile/Getty Images.
Ch3.7 Yohji Yamamoto, Runway, Paris Fashion Week, Spring/Summer 2020, photo by Victor Virgile/Getty Images.

Chapter 4

Ch4.2 Photo by AFP via Getty Images/Getty Images.

Ch4.3 Photo by Regan Vercruysse, Philadelphia Museum of Art, https://creativecommons.org/licenses/by/2.0/deed.en., available online: https://commons.wikimedia.org/wiki/File:Fabulous_Fashion_PMA(95).jpg.

Ch4.4 Photo by Keystone-France/Gamma-Rapho via Getty Images.

Ch4.5 Photo by David McCabe/Conde Nast via Getty Images.

Ch4.6 Lanvin, Runway, Paris Fashion Week, Fall/Winter 2020/2021.

Ch4.7 Gareth Pugh, Runway, London Fashion Week, September 2016, photo by Ki Price/Getty Images.

Chapter 5

Ch5.2 Scanned image from author's pattern archive.

Ch5.3 Photo by Bettmann/Getty Images.

Ch5.4 Photo by Tim Boxer/Hulton Archive/Getty Images.

Ch5.5 Photo by Victor VIRGILE/Gamma-Rapho via Getty Images.

Ch5.6 Photo by Victor VIRGILE/Gamma-Rapho via Getty Images.

Chapter 6

Ch6.2 *Madame X* (Madame Pierre Gautreau) painting by John Singer Sargent, Metropolitan Museum of Art Collection, {{PD-US}}, available online: https://commons.wikimedia.org/wiki/File:Madame_X_(Madame_Pierre_Gautreau),_John_Singer_Sargent,_1884_(unfree_frame_crop).jpg.

Ch6.3 *Theatre Magazine*, Vol. 51(5), May 1930, p. 57, photographer unknown, {{PD-US}}, available online: https://commons.wikimedia.org/wiki/File:Libby-Holman-1930.jpg.

Ch6.4 Photo by Bettmann/Getty Images.

Ch6.5 Photo by Hulton Archive/Getty Images.

Ch6.6 Rochas, Runway, Paris Fashion Week Spring/Summer 2020, photo by Victor Virgile/Getty Images.

Ch6.7 Dries Van Noten, Runway, Paris Fashion Week Spring/Summer 2020, photo by Richard Bord/Getty Images.

Chapter 7

Ch7.2 *The Modern Priscilla*, needlework magazine, 1906, artist Ethelyn J. Morris, Priscilla Publishing Co., {{PD-US}}, available online: https://commons.wikimedia.org/wiki/File:Shirtwaist_designs_1906.jpg.

Ch7.3 Imperial War Museum, photo by Division Photographer, Ministry of Information, available online: https://commons.wikimedia.org/wiki/File:How_a_British_Woman_Dresses_in_Wartime-_Utility_Clothing_in_Britain,_1943_D14784.jpg.

Ch7.4 Photo by Genevieve Naylor/Corbis via Getty Images.

Ch7.5 Photo by CBS via Getty Images/Getty Images.

Ch7.6 Celine, Runway, Paris Fashion Week, Fall/Winter 2019/2020, photo by Yanshan Zhang/Getty Images.

Ch7.6A Rochas, Runway, Paris Fashion Week, Fall/Winter 2019/2020, photo by Victor Virgile/Getty Images.

Chapter 8

Ch8.2 By an unknown nineteenth-century engraver, {{PD-US}}, available online: https://commons.wikimedia.org/wiki/File:1817-walking-dress-La-Belle-Assemblee.jpg.

Ch8.3a Photo by Nina Leen/The LIFE Picture Collection via Getty Images.

Ch8.3b Photo by Brian Kirley/Hulton Archive/Getty Images.

Ch8.4 Photo by Bob (Robert) Rice/Fairfax Media via Getty Images.

Ch8.5 Photo by Terry Fincher/Princess Diana Archive/Getty Images.

Ch8.6 Alexander McQueen, Runway, Paris Fashion Week, Fall/Winter 2019/2020, photo by Estrop/Getty Images.

Ch8.7 Saint Laurent, Runway, Paris Fashion Week, Fall/Winter 2019/2020, photo by Estrop/Getty Images.

Chapter 9

Ch9.2 Photo by Keystone/Getty Images.

Ch9.3 Photo by LMPC via Getty Images/Getty Images.

Ch9.4 Photo by 2000 USA Films/Online USA/Getty Images.

Ch9.5 Source: https://www.flickr.com/photos/lydiaxliu/20650528281/, licensed under Creative Commons Attribution 2.0 Generic, available online: https://commons.wikimedia.org/wiki/File:Met_China_Looking_Glass_1.jpg.

Ch9.6 Huishan Zhang, Runway, London Fashion Week, September 2019, photo by Estrop/Getty Images.

Ch9.7 Huishan Zhang, Runway, London Fashion Week, September 2019, photo by Joe Maher/BFC/Getty Images.